A Matter of Death and Life

A Matter of Death and Life

ALICE ALDRICH HILDEBRAND

RESOURCE *Publications* • Eugene, Oregon

A MATTER OF DEATH AND LIFE

Copyright © 2025 Alice Aldrich Hildebrand. All rights reserved. Except for brief quotations in critical publications or reviews, no part of this book may be reproduced in any manner without prior written permission from the publisher. Write: Permissions, Wipf and Stock Publishers, 199 W. 8th Ave., Suite 3, Eugene, OR 97401.

Resource Publications
An Imprint of Wipf and Stock Publishers
199 W. 8th Ave., Suite 3
Eugene, OR 97401

www.wipfandstock.com

PAPERBACK ISBN: 979-8-3852-4377-8
HARDCOVER ISBN: 979-8-3852-4378-5
EBOOK ISBN: 979-8-3852-4379-2
VERSION NUMBER 05/09/25

The Scripture quotations contained herein are from the New Revised Standard Version Bible, copyright © 1989 by the Division of Christian Education of the National Council of the Churches of Christ in the USA, and are used by permission. All rights reserved.

"Because dying, like living, is seldom neat and tidy, finding a trustworthy guide about these matters is a precious gift. Equipped with wisdom hard earned from her years as a hospital chaplain, Alice Hildebrand reflects on the challenges and benefits, the risks and joys of accompanying an aging, somewhat cantankerous, yet beloved father through to his final days. No cheap sentiment here. Only fierce tenderness and savvy encouragement to honor one's feelings, come what may."

—**Marvin M. Ellison**, Willard S. Bass Professor Emeritus of Christian Ethics, Bangor Theological Seminary

"If you are a caregiver—and many of us will be—you need this wonderfully honest memoir about caring for a fragile father in his last years. Reverend Hildebrand has not only been a caregiver, but she has also been a beloved local pastor and a hospice chaplain. She models support for oneself in very difficult times. Her memoir is a daring and intimate account that will be a solace to all caregivers."

—**Bill Henderson**, author of *Cathedral: An Illness and a Healing*

"In a moving and insightful book about caring for an elderly, dying parent, Alice Hildebrand weaves stories of faith, stories of Jesus's compassionate ministry, with stories of her own efforts to be a loving daughter, an understanding wife, and a faithful disciple. Mostly she succeeds at the task, occasionally she fails, always she relates the journey clearly, beautifully, and in a way that leads the reader to consider how they would manage if asked to travel a similar path. Rarely does one encounter writing that is this honest, so intensely self-aware, and as touching as what one confronts in *A Matter of Death and Life*."

—**Dana Douglass**, Retired Minister, Deer Isle Sunset Congregational Church, United Church of Christ

"Alice Hildebrand—poet, hospital chaplain, minister, daughter—takes us on the end-of-life journey of her father. She confronts her own mortality and the mortality of the planet in a narrative that moves back and forth between the everyday practical concerns of a caregiver to the largest questions humans can ask. Her close observations, her unflinching assessments, and her evolving faith are woven together in a compelling narrative that wrestles with the complexities of love."

—STUART KESTENBAUM, Maine Poet Laureate (2016–2021)

"I read this book very carefully, taking notes on the things that caught my attention, gave me hope, or made me cry. I found it so helpful as I face the limitations of aging and a diminished capacity for doing the things that have, throughout my life, brought me meaning and joy. It is a book to be savored—a 'sand mandala' of poetic beauty to inspire the creation of our own, even in the midst of loss and death."

—ELAINE HEWES, Pastor, Evangelical Lutheran Church in America

Dedicated to my parents, with love and gratitude

Contents

Acknowledgments | ix
Introduction | xi

1. Bring Me Your Nothing | 1
2. Stones to Bread | 11
3. The Netherworld of Loss | 22
4. Deeper into the Labyrinth | 30
5. Detach Over and Over | 34
6. So Much History | 43
7. Yet Another Morning | 48
8. Christmas and a New Year | 56
9. The Bad Mood Persists | 68
10. The Gift of Limitation | 74
11. Negative Space | 84
12. Another Turn of the Wheel | 88
13. My Own Companion on the Journey | 95
14. "All things shall perish from under the sky..." | 101
15. The Secret Place of Thunder | 107
16. The Well | 111
17. Enjoy the Now | 116
18. Just Let It Go | 123
19. Pandemic | 131
20. Since I Am Alive Right Now | 143

Bibliography | 149

Acknowledgments

MANY THANKS TO:

The editorial team at Wipf and Stock Publishers for their expertise, responsiveness, patience, and encouragement.

The many colleagues and mentors who helped me discern, first, my call to writing: Howard Roland, high school English teacher, who gave me permission to find my own voice; Bill Rosenfeld, head of the Creative Writing Department at Kirkland College, who held me accountable when I was going through a difficult time; Denise Levertov, who taught me to write in such a way that it would be sensible to the reader; Helen Yglesias, who demonstrated how to be a mother, a writer, and a generous giver to other writers; and Doris Grumbach, who encouraged me to keep going. Fellow writers Stu Kestenbaum, Elaine Hewes, Nancy Avery Dafoe, Scott Vickers, and Gwynn O'Gara. Coach and guide Gabriela Macias (Bhadra Dasi), who got me started again.

Those who helped me discern my call to ministry: Susan Davies, Marvin Ellison, Burton Throckmorton, Douglas Walrath, Rob McCall, John Swift, the members and attenders of Eggemoggin Reach Monthly Meeting of the Society of Friends (Quaker), Ministry and Counsel of Vassalboro Quarterly Meeting, and Maurice Allaire.

For strength, insight, support, and humor along the way: Dana and Anne Douglass, Ron Baard, Rosie Wohl, Kasey Grover, Vanessa Little Donaldson, Kathy Nyborg, and Susan Webster.

The medical staff I have been privileged to work alongside in four different hospitals and a home care agency, especially the nurses and medical residents who taught me everything I needed to know about patient care.

ACKNOWLEDGMENTS

Mike Belinsky and Paul McNulty, who were my dad's hospice volunteers.

The nurses of Hancock County Homecare and Hospice, and especially Nancy "The Bath Lady."

Robert Baroody, whose years of conscientious and responsive medical care for my dad helped us navigate through his aging and death.

The patients and their families whose faith, anger, courage, and grief helped me to understand my own, and to remember that I was not alone.

The attenders and members of the churches I have served, whose questions about the meaning of life helped me to find out what my own questions are, and who trusted me as their pastor.

Good friends and readers of this book Anne Cushman and Bill Henderson, who plowed through it when it was a lot longer than it is today.

The many fellow travelers I have met in the rooms of the twelve-step programs, who understand.

My best friend for over fifty years, one of my most supportive and helpful readers for all those years, Mary Dillon, without whose wisdom, humor, generosity, and role modeling as a caregiver, as well as the time she spent with my dad, I would have been lost.

My extended family of cousins, who reached out to me and to my dad and kept us connected.

My son James, his wife Emily, and their children Jack and Kate; stepson Justus Myers and his partner Juliet Squire; stepson Eben Myers, his wife Laura, and their children Sadie and Lucy. You all are the reason that the things in this book are worth saying.

My husband Allen Myers, my partner in the "Mortality Project" of our common life, who not only read multiple versions of this book and patiently walked me through the production stages, but more importantly lived it with me and my dad every step of the way.

Introduction

WHERE SHALL I BEGIN this story of my father's ending, and of the caregiving journey I took with him in his last years? Like those pictures that appear to be nothing but a sea of dots until you tilt them just so and an image emerges, my relationship with my father is submerged in minutiae, in stories, his own and others; in historical context; in the falsity and the truth of memory. In *How Emotions Are Made*, neuroscientist and psychologist Lisa Feldman Barrett writes: "The human brain is a master of deception. It creates experiences and directs actions with a magician's skill."[1] The neuroscientists tell us that, in a sense, we are all artists, all writers of fiction. The psychologists and mystics tell us that who we *think* we are is actually who we *are* in practical terms. There is no useful "objective" reality that contains our "real" selves. We have to deal with whatever we are handed by our psyches; and if what we get isn't useful, is actually harmful to our sense of well-being and our ability to function in the world, then it is up to us to do what we can to rephrase what our minds are telling us about who we are. About what we deserve. About where we have failed and where we have succeeded.

My dad knew so much about the past, of his family and of the world, and encompassed the twentieth century both with the span of his years and with his keen understanding of its culture, politics, and dramas. He knew so much and said so much about the textures and the nuances of external events, but, a man of his times, said very little about his inner world. Did he understand himself? Little scraps of conversation we had in his last years, little scraps of paper I have found since his death, on which he jotted down

---

1. Barrett, *How Emotions Are Made*, 278.

his thoughts, make me think he knew more about himself than he was usually willing to acknowledge. Who did his inner artist think he was?

Born in 1919 at the tail end of World War I, he grew up in Connecticut, lived through the Depression, graduated from college into the Marine Corps and World War II, met and married my mother, and raised me in the Cold War fifties and the Vietnam War sixties in the suburbs of New York City. His family had all the usual family stresses of their times, and some that weren't as usual, like the loss of his uncle in 1924 sailing around the world with friends in a small boat. Something, that loss or the family's memories of many other losses, conspired to make them anxious people, and my father was a very anxious man.

At the end of April 2017, I left a beloved job as a chaplain in a large hospital, 150 miles away from the community in which my dad had lived since retirement in 1986 and in which I had lived since 1978, to help him. He was then a healthy ninety-seven-year-old, but he was increasingly running up against limitations. I had commuted to this job weekly for six years (coming home on weekends), and during those years my husband Allen had been cooking supper, helping with yard work, and giving Dad rides to doctor's appointments in Bangor, fifty miles away, while I was away each week and as Allen wound down his own career. But now Dad's doctor didn't want him driving at all, even on our nearly empty country roads. No more trips to the post office or the library, no more grocery shopping or volunteer work. As my dad changed, what he needed began to seem to me like it would be too much to ask of Allen. And Allen's end-of-career job was one he loved, as summer minister on an offshore island; this year Dad couldn't be alone week after week while Allen and I were both away.

I came home to help my dad, and to be with him and Allen, but I also came home because I had painted myself into a corner at the job I loved so well. I came home in shock from having made the decision to end my beloved career as a pediatric chaplain because my relationship with my boss had become so conflictual and stressful that it wasn't worth it to me anymore. I loved my dad and my husband and I wanted to be with them. But as I woke up each day to the prospect of an unstructured day until it was time to cook supper, albeit a day in an absolutely beautiful place by the sea in the tiny village of Brooklin, Maine, I missed my work at the hospital terribly.

I missed the fast pace of a level one trauma center and children's hospital. I felt discontented and restless. I was grieving—a loss of a self, of the person I had been at that job, of the things I was accomplishing there, of my plans for futures. I knew intellectually that I was also, somehow, somewhere in my heart, carrying the losses I had been through there, as a companion to many, many patients and families and staff members. I wasn't ready to truly feel those losses yet. I brooded about who I was going to be now without that work and reflected a lot about loss—disappointments, endings, little "deaths" that occur throughout life—the deaths of dreams, hopes, ambitions, plans. I looked with hostility at my own projections of empty months adding up to empty years.

Even as I wallowed in these feelings, I did expect that I would come to terms with them. I'm a pragmatic person and I needed to earn my living. A local church of my denomination, the United Church of Christ, was searching for a part-time pastor; it was a church I knew well as my husband had previously served it for five and a half years. They were happy to call us as a couple and I returned to parish ministry in the most welcoming setting I could have imagined. It seemed there would be a new order to my life after all, and one that would allow for plenty of spiritual reflection and growth.

However, when I had been home for only a few weeks, my dad got pneumonia and nearly died. When he was released from the local hospital, his level of functioning had deteriorated significantly. He couldn't walk without a walker for the first time in his life. Even with the walker he couldn't safely walk on his own for more than a few steps. He couldn't stand at the stove and stir his own oatmeal and morning cocoa. He couldn't carry a container of yogurt, a spoon, and a glass of ginger ale to the table for lunch while managing his walker. The distance from his bed to the bathroom was impossibly long so he had to accept having a commode in his room for nighttime. There was a multitude of things he couldn't do at all, and of things that he had to do differently. Each day we learned more about his new limitations and losses. He would never be able to live alone again. Never a sanguine person, he was angry and sad, day after day.

And me? Instead of having the luxury to sort and sift and grieve the changes in my professional life, to sit on the porch and stare at the dawn at our family's small seaside cabin seven miles away, where Allen and I had lived off and on for several years, I was at my dad's house. Allen and I moved into the upstairs there, he left for the first week of his summer job, and I was challenged to live at the rhythm of Dad's needs rather than my own. I had helped to take care of my mother when she was a home hospice patient twenty years before, so I knew the territory. I thought. I had yet to learn that, since I am an only child, this second death would feel totally

Introduction

different. It would mean the end of my original family forever. I had yet to learn the profound dislocations within helping my complex, elusive father live out his dying.

Living in his house with him meant living in a complicated web of the present, the imagined past, the remembered past, and the past lost to conscious thought but powerfully contributing to every moment in the here and now. I had struggled for forty-eight or so years—since I left home to go to college—to keep all of that safely confined to my journal and to conversations with close friends, with my husband, with my therapist. Safely confined except for times like vacations with my parents, weekend visits with them, and a few brief attempts to live with my dad right after my mother died of lung cancer in 1997. Safely confined except for nearly every encounter I'd had with my dad once I began to be self-aware instead of just rebellious.

When was that? Maybe not until I got sober at age thirty-two. Or maybe, conversely, when I began to drink and use drugs at age ten. Maybe even before that, at age nine, when I began smoking cigarettes. Maybe even before *that*, when the four-year-old me—who would become a latchkey kid with working parents at age five after half-day kindergarten—ran away to the neighbors' house looking for company in the little girl living there who was the same age as me, but even more so in that little girl's mother. Maybe I was never "just rebellious" but always self-aware, and, therefore, always aware of both my need for nurture and my fear of being so nurtured, so anxiously tended, that I would smother. My mother appeared to be psychologically absent much of the time, although she could also be charming, fascinating, larger-than-life. She was, I believe, an alcoholic, albeit a high-functioning one. My dad was attentive, patient, loving—but also fearful and clingy, wanting to be reassured one moment and advised by me the next.

An ancient Christian formulation from the Book of Common Prayer[2] burial liturgy affirms, "In the midst of life, we are in death." A good reminder that we can never assume a lengthy future for ourselves or anyone or, indeed, anything, but ought to live in the awareness of inevitable ending. But one could also say, on a cellular level, that in the midst of death, we are in life—new cells are made as old ones die, right up to the moment when the entire body gets the message that there is no blood coming from the heart anymore, no electricity coming from the brain. One could say, on an emotional level, that in the midst of death, we are in life—opportunities expanding all around us as we grow and change, even as things end. We learn and forget and readjust and calculate.

2. Episcopal Church, *Book of Common Prayer*, 484.

Introduction

And so, I realized gradually, as I adjusted to days that were now defined not by journaling and meditating and reflecting on all that was bound up in my choice to end my chaplaincy career, but by caregiving, that the small endings within the choice—ending of an identity, ending of relationships, ending of projects, ending of service to others in a particular place—were *nothing* like the ending that is actual death. I realized that the loss of a beloved career is actually about life, not about death, as it is part of moving forward, part of new opportunities for gains and growth in self-knowledge, in creativity, in vision. And then I also realized that caregiving itself, with all its repetitive wearying stress, was also about life. That my dad as he declined was still living, and that I was living with him.

I decided that I needed to write each day as best I could, to mark the days, to still feel like a self. From those writings this book emerged. It is an offering to you who are caregivers now, or have been caregivers, or will be caregivers in the future, which means this book is probably for us all.

1

Bring Me Your Nothing

2017

DAD IS IN THE hospital with pneumonia. When he took sick, I briefly considered whether we should keep him at home to die, whether that was what we were supposed to do with someone who was very clear about his doctors taking "no heroic measures" to save his life. I ran that by my son James, a physician specializing in emergency medicine, and he pointed out that for Dad, who has no underlying health conditions, just old, old age, pneumonia is an easily treatable condition. Going to the hospital is not a heroic measure in his case, but appropriate care.

While Dad is safely there and under someone else's supervision, I watch the fields behind his house turn slowly green, I watch as the wildflowers appear, the rhodora blooming on the roadsides, then the lupine in the meadows. I know that next will come the buttercups and clover and daisies of June. The daylilies and heliotrope of July. By August, it will all be black-eyed Susans and goldenrod, giving way to the asters of September. I've marked this progression of the flowers for many years, been aware of the changing time of sunrise and of how the sun slides northward then back toward the south. I've watched the phases of the moon and known the names of the birds as they arrive and leave and arrive again. It's all change. Nothing is fixed in place. Except memory.

A Matter of Death and Life

***

True enough, going to the hospital is not a heroic measure for Dad. He bounces back after twenty-four hours of antibiotics and comes home after only a week. He is well medically, he is alert and focused as ever mentally, but he is frail physically. He needs a walker for the first time in his life, and that really changes things. I'm not going to be able to just be a companion to my dad, I'm going to be a caregiver.

One morning after a month of trying, I get him to agree to let a certified nursing assistant from the Visiting Nurse Association help him take a shower. It takes bullying, cajoling, and even letting him win for a while before he finally admits that trying to do it by himself is exhausting and makes him feel unsafe. But by the time she actually shows up, he has forgotten about our agreement and begins to fuss and say no all over again.

I give up the idea of leaving the house to take a break while she is here, despite her urging, because I am afraid that if I leave the shower won't happen. It would be easier just to let him go unwashed, but that wouldn't be good caregiving. I think.

***

The disciples say to Jesus, "This is a deserted place, and the hour is now late; send the crowds away so that they may go into the villages and buy food for themselves." Send the crowds away! Their need is so great and our resources so small.

They had started the day with the horrifying news that King Herod had beheaded John the Baptist. They put their grief aside to help Jesus with hordes of needy people all day long. Now, exhausted and concerned about getting everybody fed, they have come up with a solution: Let them fend for themselves. There are so many needs!

Jesus says, "They need not go away; you give them something to eat."

They reply in consternation, "We have nothing here but five loaves and two fish."

He answers, "Bring them here to me."[1] Bring me your nothing.

Taking the five loaves and the two fish, he looks up to heaven and blesses and breaks the loaves, gives them to the disciples and the disciples give them to the crowds. They're tired, they're hungry themselves, but they make their way along the rows of waiting people, resigned, puzzled at why

---

1. Matt 14:15b–18.

Jesus is doing this odd thing, feeling bad for all those whose bellies will still be empty when the small supply of bread and fish runs out . . . mechanically reaching in and taking up pieces of bread and fish over and over . . . and over and over . . . and with quickening hearts realizing that they have fed ten people, then twenty, then one hundred, and still, each time they reach into the baskets for another portion of bread and fish, there is more . . .

***

When I can steal a few hours of quiet and space to myself, usually at our cabin by the sea, I am nervous, slightly guilty, all too ready to go back to my dad's house and start supper early. All too ready to bring not my nothing but my *something*. This is why I matter. This is what buys me a place on the planet. This is what staves off emptiness and meaninglessness. I can cook some string beans. I can set the table. I can clean up.

Bring me your nothing, my heart says to me. To my discontented, irritable self.

"Bring me your nothing," Jesus says. "Bring me your inadequacy, your emptiness, your brokenness, your fears, your helplessness, your sadness, your guilt—bring your nothing to me.

"Bring your nothing to me and I will receive your nothing and bless it and break it and feed the world with what you have brought. I will bless you and break you and make you whole again. I will show you how to make something from nothing, by the simple power of love."

Was that what Jesus was talking about in the story of the loaves and fishes? Somehow I think there is more here in this scripture than there is in any charitable act of feeding the hungry. Yes, it is vitally important that while I figure out the state of my soul, people get fed, have housing, stay warm. But what else is going on here in this passage? Feed the world with your broken, inadequate soul. The world is very hungry. The needs are enormous and you are very small—but, "Feed the world."

But what feeds my soul? Jesus, if he was even a real person, was surely not talking about self-care the way we read about it in contemporary magazines. He, or at least Matthew and the other Gospel writers, was talking about care for one another and how God wants and expects that of us. It's twenty-first-century sleight of hand to take these ancient texts and make them be about *my* needs. I don't need loaves or fishes. I have a supermarket nearby full of food—but I am oh so very hungry in other ways.

Jesus wasn't talking about self-care, but he *was* talking about putting God and our neighbors at the center of our lives would give us better lives. And would help us give the whole world better lives. *Bring me your nothing.* Like everything else in the universe we are integral parts of creation; we are something. Physicists tell us that the molecules of our breath influence the winds that circle the globe, as do the great ocean currents. But at least as far as we know, the molecules of our breath and the great ocean currents have no self-awareness in the way that we do, no capacity to be anxious about their own power. It is not enough for us to know that we are no less important than sun and moon and stars. We want to know that we are more. More valuable, more loved. More loved by God, who is only love, and in whom there are no gradations.

Long ago, my New Testament professor warned us never to put the word *love* in a sermon unless the biblical scripture from which we were preaching also contained that word. Why? Maybe because talking about love is a cheap way to feed your audience. Sure, it gets everyone fed for at least that one moment. But sentimentality is not ultimately sustaining.

Jesus didn't feed people cheaply. If he is really my teacher, then what do I need to learn from him about feeding others? About feeding myself? About caring for my father in this new phase of our life together, a task for which I feel so inadequate.

***

Leaving my job as a hospital chaplain was a many-months decision because I was not ready to leave. Not ready to be done with my career and not ready to abandon projects like perinatal palliative care, and whole-family care for parents of newborn babies affected by the mom's drug use during pregnancy. Not ready to leave partnering with the leaders of the Muslim community to educate hospital staff about Muslim burial customs. Not ready to leave working with staff on their own needs for self-care. But thoroughly sick of and exhausted by institutional politics. So, I was ready to go despite being afraid that I wouldn't be able to find anything to do back at home that would be as meaningful as what I had been doing as a chaplain.

But, as I thought more about it, I realized that being involved with Allen, my husband, my lab partner in this experiment with no control group called *life*, in what I term the *mortality project*, was plenty meaningful. The mortality project—coming to terms with my own death, with how each vivid, lacerating, or awe-inspiring moment, or all of them, even the ones that do not feel exceptional in any way, is a breath surrounded by the potential and promised end of breath.

The mortality project is the work that it takes to understand how to live while dying. To understand that this is our state, from day one. Change. To understand that there is no way to keep our life options perpetually open, or at least not all of them. The self we know physically, mentally, and emotionally is changing all the time into someone we might not want to be—first to an older person, and then to a much older person. An *old* old person. A possibly frail old person. Time closes off options, even while we cling to our memories of who we "always" have been.

Time also adds new ones, and maybe we don't like these new ones so well, since they include things like adjusting to waning abilities and power. But while we, in our fear of choice-making or commitment or mortality itself, may work to be a perpetual ingénue, an always promising beginner, we are aging.

And in thinking about my dad, a very private person steeped in literature, the arts, history, politics, who always cared about the well-being and aspiration of all people, and who would talk about that so readily yet about himself not much at all; and in thinking about all the end-of-life conversations I have had with folks over the years, some explicitly meaning-making about the Big Picture, but more of them about the little pictures that make up our days—it seems to me that, in a way, death is an aspect of culture. In our aging and approach to death, we lose our sense of location in the things that define us on the knowable surface of our lives. Yes, there is a biological end point for everything that lives, but what we reflect on when we contemplate death is not really that unfathomable end point but its meaning, and that is defined for us by our context and our culture.

T. S. Eliot, Joseph Conrad, William Shakespeare, James Joyce, and many other writers; paintings, ballet, and most of all opera—these have been my dad's sources of transcendence, I think. And as his physical energy wanes, he is losing those things, at least in the way he used to have them, a vital, relational way. They still must be in his head somewhere, but do they still texture and give meaning to his time? Death is not just the end of a biological life but the loss of things that are meaningful even while we are very much alive biologically.

I came home in the throes of a death of my own—the death of my sense of self as a hospital chaplain. I came home wanting to make sense of the losses I experienced in my career—which occurred on several levels.

For some reason, what might seem to be the most obvious stimulation of thought about death and loss, the fact of death as a daily occurrence in the hospital, remained in the background for me. The death in the foreground was the loss of my profession, the loss of opportunities for delight as I exercised professional power, as I accomplished important things—little ones for individual patients, big ones in influencing institutional policy and process. What died was an important part of my own construction of the meaning of my life.

I had some very negative experiences as part of a huge institution. Someone took credit for my research work. Someone lied about me. Someone abused their power. Someone ignored my ideas. Someone manipulated me. So what? None of that ever stopped me from doing my job with patients and families and staff, doing it well. I left that place with a yearning for some sort of justice/restitution, which felt out of proportion to the events that had actually happened, so what was really going on in me? What actually died? That was what I expected to work on at home while I was being a companion rather than a caregiver to my dad.

I acknowledged my disproportionate sense of woundedness about aspects of the way I was treated at the hospital. My yearning for vindication, for wrongs righted, for bad guys punished and good guys rewarded is rooted in woundedness from my childhood, I believe, where I so often had to struggle alone with adult behavior that made no sense to me. And I believe that addressing a sense of childhood woundedness is a developmental imperative, work that has to be done by anyone who wants to grow into emotionally mature adulthood. In that sense, grieving the psychic deaths of ambitions, of hopes and dreams and plans, is an ongoing process that is way more important than grieving our own physical death, at least until we truly realize we are dying.

Death in the aggregate—the death of my patients, the death of the millions, death as my own eventual biological end point—is a concept to mull. Psychologists tell us that the mulling of concepts belongs to a mature stage of consciousness; it's an adult activity. Mulling can be a way to connect with other humans, at least intellectually. We locate ourselves within the stream of history and culture. And rehearsing death with others is perhaps a way to explore what it means to cease to be. But the unmet needs of childhood are not merely concepts to mull, they are integral to who we are and will get tangled up in all our adult activities, all our adult awareness, if we don't get them sorted out.

I believed strongly that continuing to work on my childhood stuff was the most important task I had to do when I arrived home. I expected that I would have a lot of opportunities to learn about boundaries, limits, forgiveness, forbearance. I could see in myself a kind of loneliness that I also identified in my dad. Dad wanted my presence at his side in an insatiable way that went beyond any physical needs for help. His need for my attention was overwhelming.

According to the therapist I had for many years, and I believe her on this, we are entitled to get that kind of attention from others when we are infants because we are helpless and we need it in order to survive. But after that phase we can only legitimately get round-the-clock nurturing attention from ourselves. If we didn't get enough parental presence when we were infants, as adults we are going to have to learn how to make up for that—to parent ourselves. And we will all, ultimately, have to comfort ourselves alone in the final night of our dying, no matter how many beloveds walk with us up to the threshold. We will step over it alone. No magic. My dad was drawing nearer to that threshold.

***

Today, I have stolen some time for myself. Right now Allen is ashore for a few days, on a break from his summer job on the island, and can be with Dad. Having some time alone is even more important than being with Allen. When he is away, we can talk on the phone at night, each on our islands—his, a physical, real island five miles offshore. Mine, the island of caregiving, offshore from the easy coming-and-going interchanges of adult, able-bodied life. All that mobility and power of choice that is so easy to take for granted until it is curtailed. Then see how connected you feel. Then see whether or not there is a land bridge to discover once the tide is out.

So, for a few days I am sleeping in the cabin and awakening to the sky-wide hum of lobster boats, which make the bed I lie in throb with their sound. The sky is rose colored, then blinding white and blue in the brilliant east as the sun rises, and cloudless and pure in the west where the moon grows pale as it sinks behind the ancient apple tree on the brow of the hill, the apple tree in the photographs my great-grandmother took in 1910.

It will be another hot day, as yet no breezes blowing, and the windows of the cabin, still cool from the night, are masked with droplets of water. In an hour, the boats will have gone off to deeper ocean and the air will be absolutely still, silence not broken even by the caws of crows or the shrieks of the seagulls at rest on the low tide bar where the rocks are heaped with tawny weed, dotted around the tide pools where barnacles feed.

I sit in the still-cool cabin, in the quiet, with the growl of the boats receding, growing fainter, and the field around me that was lupine two months ago gone to tansy now. I have no radio, no television, no internet here, so I don't know whether we are at war with North Korea, Russia, Iran, or just with ourselves. The man in the White House and his advisors seem as self-centered, immature, and unwise as any of the empire builders of the past. Those builders of empire affected, controlled, upended the lives of the little people, but empire builders eventually come to the end of their powers, through defeat, through death. Just like little people.

***

On the last day of my stolen break from caregiving, I come back to Dad's house, to Allen, in the middle of the night. Something awakened me and before I knew it I slid down into the pit of sadness and fear that I think of as residue from childhood, and didn't want to be alone with my thoughts. Good therapy has helped me to come to believe that the reason those feelings are so overwhelming is that they're from that time when I was easily overwhelmed, had no power—the years of childhood. I have pondered; what was it like to lie in my bed at home, my bedroom painted pink, with pink bedspread and curtains, and feel so afraid? I can remember being terrified of the dark, of witches that could climb the walls of our house and snatch me from my bed. I have no reason to think that "something" happened to me, just memories of being afraid.

Today's bad time started at supper, for which I had left my retreat at the cabin and joined Allen and Dad briefly. I had had a wonderful, whole-feeling day—the kind of day that is my absolute favorite, in which I had no structure but my own, and could read my book for pleasure, my book for serious thought, write in my journal, do some reflecting on caregiving, take a walk, stare at the ocean, go to the farmers market, tidy the house. All the pieces of a day done at leisure, without having to be rationed.

Allen is always fully supportive of me getting this kind of chance for me to be *me* on my own. He and I routinely divide up the chores, get all the jobs done. But after supper this evening—which I had planned and Allen cooked, as is our frequent arrangement—as he was out watering the garden, which I have done quite a lot this dry summer, hauling the long, heavy hose all the way out to the garden and standing amid the mosquitos until there are puddles softening the tight soil around our plants, Dad said, "We should do the dishes. Allen has done so much." And I was instantly furious, even as I was planning, of course, to do the dishes, which is my job at night; furious in a way I so often, so quickly become around my dad.

The surface idea: Stay out of my relationship with my husband. More surface: You don't tell Allen to wash the dishes when *I* have "done so much." My dad does usually thank me, but in a way that doesn't seem grateful as much as it seems guilty. Guilty for not doing the cooking or the cleaning himself. The deeper ideas: Why do you, Dad, always expect me to be an extension of you instead of being myself, to do what you think is right, to carry out your program? And, why is it so hard for me to trust your expressions of gratitude, to Allen or to me, but to always feel manipulated?

Maybe Dad is truly grateful when he thanks me. But it feels somehow dangerous. I feel instantly squirrelly, embarrassed, like I want to get away. It's too late for this. Just as my occasionally outsized yearning for love and affirmation is a leftover from childhood, a need that will never be fillable by anyone but me now in adulthood, so is my need for space. Throughout my life that need for space has trumped all of my other needs, leading me into impossible relationships with unavailable people time and time again, although now, thanks to the genuine miracle of twelve-step recovery, therapy, and a lot of hard work, I have a solid marriage of many years and a lot of good friends.

When I get mad about Dad's comment regarding the dishes, I make things worse for myself by flaring up at him and then feeling guilty. Such an old pattern in my life with my dad. The first time I ever got any inkling that there could be relief from this seemingly perpetual pattern of anger and then guilt and regret followed by blame and self-blame was when, in a medical presentation, I heard the phrase "the family illness of alcoholism." So many of the behaviors and attitudes the presenter went on to describe fit my memories of childhood perfectly. Attributes of my character that I thought were unique to me were laid out in an austere medical chart as typical of those living in homes with an alcoholic parent. That moment might have been the first time I ever really acknowledged to myself that my mother had more than "a drinking problem." I said to myself for the first time, *I have been shaped and damaged by growing up in a family with an alcoholic parent, and with an anxious, "co-alcoholic" co-parent.*

After I snap at my dad, help him to his easy chair, get the news on on the television, and do the dishes, as soon as Allen is back inside, seething I head back to the cabin. I turn to an Al-Anon book, desperately opening it at random, hoping for something that will point me toward calm and relief. I read a description of various constructive ways to respond to someone else's behavior—and then see this: "It is not our goal to be 'right.' It is not our goal to 'win.' Our goal is to do everything we can to heal ourselves and our relationships."[2] And I realize with shock that I do not want to heal my relationship with my dad. I *want* to win. I want to overpower.

Last week's revelation, in two parts, was, first: *I need to just put all my energy into making my father happy.* Then: *Oh my God, how could I still fall for that? I can't* make *him happy!* This week's revelation is, first, that I still want to prove something to my father about my worth. I still want finally to be right. And then, thankfully, I've realized yet again, that there is no way to do that, either. Healing my relationship with Dad doesn't have to mean actually healing that relationship in real time, or with him. It can mean—in fact, it can only mean—healing that relationship inside myself.

A big twelve-step program word is *detachment*. Maybe that could be a middle way for this time—not the self-denial of making him my only focus, and not the disregard of him that would make me my only focus either. But a balance between his needs and my own. There is the option of detaching from his neediness without detaching from his needs.

Though this will require me to address the challenge of figuring out what my needs and his needs actually are.

---

2. *How Al-Anon Works*, 31.

2

Stones to Bread

A FOGGY, RAINY MORNING after a night of rain, welcome in this dry summer. And for once Dad is still sleeping when I am awake. Awake, aware in this house with all its objects. Furniture, paintings, boxes of letters. This house is so close to smothering me all the time, and suddenly gets much smaller when he is awake in it, too. The heavily curtained windows, the shades drawn halfway down. Once upon a time I felt responsible for the proper stewardship of all of this, felt that after he died I would spend years making sure that nothing in this house was carelessly disposed of, and that I would review every scrap of saved writing, every photograph, and the four generations of children's drawings. Now I think it will not be hard at all to give much of it a cursory glance and throw it away. I think this is partly because I am aging and thus am more aware of my own mortality and the brevity of my time. But it is also because I am less in thrall to Dad and to the past. Just because all these things have been important to him, and were important to his grandmother and his father and his Aunt Alice, doesn't mean they have to be important to me.

**

My father so rarely has spoken of his feelings—yet, I have felt his feelings my whole remembered life, and probably did in my unremembered, preverbal infant life too. His feelings have been such a huge part of the construction of *my* feelings. Which of course is true for any child of any parent, but in a small family like mine, with two parents and one child, and with all the "unspeakingness" of WASP culture, combined with alcoholism, there was so little coming in from the outside world to balance the information coming in from my parents' worlds. That's probably true for more children than not; children don't know what is "normal."

How slowly it dawned on me that my family life was unhappy. There may not actually be such a thing as normal family life, but some families are certainly happier than others. Even more slowly, it dawned on me that all my years of acting out—which were really quite tame compared to some people's, yet so consistent that they added up to a fairly big dysfunctionality—were fueled by anger at my parents, at my childhood life. And by my enormous anxiety.

I came home on the school bus from half-day kindergarten and walked into an empty house to look for a snack. This was in the 1950s in a sleepy little village, but it is scary to come home to an empty house when you are five years old. My dad was whisked away on the commuter train to his office in Manhattan every morning and came home at nearly my bedtime each night. My mom was a school nurse at the local high school but she got home three or four hours later than me. I was alone.

***

There have been several days, a week or more, in which I haven't written, haven't kept my basic minimal commitment to myself to write a page a day. It is so hard to write when I feel myself up against the backdrop of mortality—read *futility*. Yesterday in a session with my therapist, she made a useful distinction between the way I described my goals when I was an active addict—to seek a kind of perpetual sparkle, from an external source, capable of lifting me out of myself and into a different reality—and what she termed "savor." "Sparkle" to me means revved-up excitement, "savor" means calm absorption. She was using food addiction as an example—probably the most obvious instance of a problem with savor. There is a big difference between inhaling food almost without noticing its flavor, and actually tasting it. How many times have I eaten, or watched someone else eat, a delicious food, even chocolate, in such a hurried way as to not experience the pleasure of its uniqueness at all? And it occurred to me that I could think of savoring the experience of my father's end of life and his dying. Not in the sense of "enjoying" but in the sense of actually tasting, actually experiencing, instead of anxiously jumping around in my days and in my feelings. To make space for myself in amongst the demands of caregiving.

I don't really know what that would be like, as I begin this new, deeper involvement in my dad's life. It might or might not mean spending more time with him. It might or might not mean asking to hear stories or identifying people in old pictures, sitting side by side looking over family things saved since the 1700s. Actually, when I reflect on my mother's death twenty years ago, I remember how much I wished, after she was dead, that I had done more of that, and yet at the same time I knew that I couldn't have, really; it was too exhausting to care for her, and about her, and also to go to work and care for my own family.

Eventually, in my work as chaplain in hospice and at the hospital, I came to believe that looking at our interactions with a dying beloved and regretting some aspect of those interactions is a normal and common part of grieving. It has to do with control as much as it has to do with yearning. We think, if only I had done X, then . . . ("Then" what? It wouldn't hurt so much? It wouldn't have happened at all?) Now twenty years closer to my own death, I am even more aware of the limits to what one can do as a caregiver while losing a beloved. There are limits to what I want to take from my dad, however much he wants to impart to me his sense of what is important so that I can carry it on—which mostly seems to be an obligation to be worried and overwhelmed, anyway.

Savoring his death might just mean being aware of and forgiving my edginess and unhappiness; again, not in the sense of enjoying, but in the sense of actually tasting, knowing what the flavors are. Reminding myself to pay attention to all that occurs in this time instead of trying to rush through it, even if it doesn't mean that I actually do anything differently.

For me, writing is a kind of savoring. It demands a slow pace most of the time, even though what I want is a rapid flow of inspiration so that the words leap onto the page. I remember writing poetry in that way when I was drunk, so many years ago in college. But even then, in order for a poem to be worth anything it had to be revised, and that was a slow process, one that I did learn to willingly engage in and love in a different way from the rush of writing the first draft. It wasn't until later, when I became briefly a Communist and felt that art was essentially suspect as it fed no one, housed no one, and changed no one's living condition (I wouldn't say that anymore) that my writing began to stall.

At that point in my life, I felt guilty about writing, so I stole my writing time like stealing bits of bread and butter while on a diet. Wolfing them down, so they won't really count. Scrabbling first drafts into my journal over and over. Later on, as I continued to edge my way into an adult world of responsibility, at the same time that my drinking and my drug use were becoming more and more a habit, a coping mechanism, and less and less an adventure, writing made space for a vulnerability that I couldn't afford. I was trying to be married to a man who really had no interest in me except when he was yelling at me; and then he left, we divorced, and I was a single parent. The savoring pace of anything was lost in a blur of tasks.

***

My dad seems to be stable, albeit a stability of a very unstable sort. I am feeling as if I will go crazy if I don't find some kind of meaningful work to do. Something more than housework and tending to him. Something more absorbing than the very part-time work I do for the very small church I now pastor quarter-time with my husband—even though I am extremely grateful for that work. I love writing and preaching a sermon. But I feel all dressed up with nowhere to go on many of my days.

In one sense, I look back at the six years at the hospital that just ended and see my pleasure at the intensity of that work as an addiction. As long as I was busy with the smorgasbord of need there, I was distracted from my anxiety. When I was juggling my work with patients, my work with staff, and my work with others in the spiritual care department on a research project or various quality improvement projects, I could always find something to do. But to do all that really only served as a distraction from the other task. This task of landing in my life and *being* there, of laying anxious striving to rest. Savoring.

I am glad that I evidently did some good for others while I was thrashing around. But it was the same phenomenon on a six-year scale as the feeling I can have at the end of one day, no matter how many people I have seen, talked to, been with. When the door of my room at last closes and the world is shut out, I can feel as if am in an empty and desolate wilderness. "In the midst of life, we are in death." Death of our spirit, death of our soul, can easily happen while we are so very, very busy with our frantic lives.

A month and a half ago when I started this writing, I thought I was observing my own passage to the end of my dad's life. Now it feels more like a kind of *No Exit*, Jean-Paul Sartre's play about hell, in which trapped people tear each other apart eternally. Family living. At the worst moments when, because Dad doesn't have his hearing aids in, I have to raise my voice really loudly, and then, because I am already irritated at having been interrupted by someone who can't hear me, when I try to find out what he needs or wants, I scream, and the very act of screaming makes me even more irritated.

I angrily say, "Why don't you put your hearing aids in before you call me," or "Stop calling me when you can't hear what I say," or just, "*What?*"

Periodically I remind myself that the bottom line, the one thing I am totally successful at with him so far, is that I am making it possible for him to stay in his own home. He's not in a nursing home where he would languish in a sea of game shows and Fox News. If I don't do anything else for him, I am doing this. And of course, doing it with the full knowledge that I could make this big investment and rearrange my life to make it possible, enlist my husband, my son, and my best friend Mary to help, and he could still end up there.

And always in the shadows, I'm wondering, *what will my end of life be?*

Well, that is a lot of uncertainty. One thing I know right now is that I have got to stay in the moment with all of this stuff. For today, we are here at my dad's house and I have made myself a workspace upstairs with my husband's help. And my son has given us a headset for the television, which means Dad can listen to his endless MSNBC news without me hearing it.

Stay in the moment and work to be grateful for what is, Alice. Which is the best antidote for anxiety, too. Don't project, and practice gratitude.

***

> Then Jesus was led up by the Spirit into the wilderness to be tempted by the devil. He fasted forty days and forty nights, and afterwards he was famished. The tempter came and said to him, "If you are the Son of God, command these stones to become loaves of bread." But he answered, "It is written, 'One does not live by bread alone, but by every word that comes from the mouth of God.'"[1]

How tempting it is to turn stones to bread. And there is a lot of bustling and doing in the Gospels. Easy to miss all those places where Jesus withdraws to be alone and pray. When I was training to be a chaplain, I thought a lot about this scripture. A basic unit of Clinical Pastoral Education is a part of many ministers' training. You learn what it is like to visit people when they

---

1. Matt 4:1–4.

are extremely ill, or when they are close to death, and what it is like to visit with the families of these people. You learn how to spend time with the nurses and doctors who work to cure them or to at least make their passage to death more comfortable. You learn the technical details of many kinds of illness and injury. But most of all, you learn about yourself.

As a chaplain resident, I spent a year in training, and boy did I learn a lot about myself. The training center I went to, a large hospital in urban Connecticut, at that time had 955 beds. When you add staff and visitors, you have a community with a larger population than any of the towns on the peninsula where I live today, about four thousand at any given time. A population gathered together with common hopes to heal, or to be healed. Within that hospital was always an extreme intensity of human hope, human need.

We chaplains spent our time in the intensive care units, the emergency room, and the surgical waiting rooms. We rarely visited with the folks who were there for a minor thing like an appendectomy or the joyous occasion of a birth. We went from one desperate situation to another. My units were the neurotrauma floor and its ICU, and the pediatric floor and its ICU. Most of my patients, no matter their ages, were not going to be able to live the lives that they had previously lived or that had been dreamed of for them. Many of them died.

All of us—the doctors, the nurses, the families, I myself—all of us wanted to be able to turn stones to bread. To change the rules of the diseases, of the injuries. With the best of intentions, with hearts full of love and caring, we wanted to change the physical universe from the way it is to the way we thought it ought to be. We longed to offer reassurances that the laws of the physical world, the laws by which the universe is ordered, were going to be overturned on behalf of our patients. Miracles do happen. Yes, there sometimes are inexplicable cures, spontaneous remissions. But it is not our job to offer them as much as we may want to. I learned this over and over as a chaplain. Family caregivers learn it too.

It's not a bad motive, but it misses the point. The task for nonmedical folks like chaplains or family caregivers and friends is to be present with people in their suffering—truly and deeply present. And that can be very hard. We cannot fix things for people, no matter how much they deserve different situations, no matter how much we care. But we can be present. Just show up and be consistent.

When I was a chaplain, I learned that I wanted to help end people's suffering not only because I cared about them, but because it met a need of mine not to see them in pain. I wanted to have the universe be different so that all its pain and untimely death and chaos would go away. Slowly I learned instead to try to embrace the mystery of our situation as very vulnerable, very small creatures who belong here, who have a right to be here, who are valuable.

A second temptation described in the Gospel accounts[2] can be applied to our lives and understood as an invitation to ignore our own safety, mental and physical, and our needs for sleep, for renewal, for food, for recreation, and for rest as well as for work. We think, "I am so important to the lives of all these people that I must never rest. They depend on me. If I push myself past my limits, it will be okay, because I'm doing God's work and God will bail me out. God won't let me crash and burn. God won't let me injure myself no matter how un-self-caring I am."

And the third temptation described by Matthew[3] touches on our desires to be so good at what we do that the whole world will be stunned and admiring. If we cannot change people's situations, perhaps we can be so good at our faithfulness to them, and to our acts of mercy and loving kindness, that everyone will admire us. We may actually turn away from human need to feed upon that admiration, that adulation. What good people we are! Many of the Scriptures tell us to let our acts of faithfulness be done in secret, whether they be fasting and praying, or the giving of charity to the poor. How easy it is, how very human, to wish to be the center of attention.[4]

***

Last night at bedtime, already in bed with his hearing aids out, Dad said, "I have to think about how I am going to live." I assumed we were going to go to a place we have gone before where he annoyingly makes the assumption that he is going to be on his own, that I am going to leave for my own pursuits. But fortunately, I did not respond crossly or dismissively, just was able to listen.

"What do you mean?"

2. Matt 4:5.

3. Matt 4:8.

4. These reflections on the theme of the temptations of Jesus in the desert were inspired by a long-ago lecture given by Rev. Douglas A. Walrath at Bangor Theological Seminary.

"I have all these people coming in to help me with my physical needs." (Again, I made the assumption that he was about to talk about how he needed to be independent, that the time was coming when the home nursing service would discharge him and be done and he would be alone. But again, fortunately, I was able to be silent.) "But what about my mind?" (Does he mean decisions, is he worrying about the checkbook again? Or the windows in the living room that are fine but which he thinks need repair, and how to get that done? Or, most out of character, does he mean feelings?)

"Do you mean your emotional mind or your powers of reason?"

"Emotion. I can't spend the remaining months of my life sitting in that chair reading *The New Yorker*."

Wow. An opening. Not for that moment, at bedtime, with the hearing aids out. But for some time, soon. To talk about death, his death. And life. And meaning.

"You could write your memoirs . . . when I was sorting boxes today, I came across stuff that Uncle Bob and Uncle Art wrote about their lives. Not great writing . . . you wouldn't have to worry about that, but just about getting things down. Or you could go back to reading T. S. Eliot . . . or Dylan Thomas . . ." (He smiles.) "Or Shakespeare."

"Yes, I've been thinking about reading Shakespeare. I'll think about it tomorrow. Maybe by morning this will have figured itself out."

True to form, back into his hidey-hole—but still, an opening, perhaps.

I cannot turn stones to bread for my father, as much as I love him. I cannot take his life which he vaguely describes as full of missed opportunities, wrong turns, failures of nerve and will, and make it into a rich and satisfying whole. The little girl still within me, who was taught so early on to make his happiness her job, still thinks that, actually, she *can* do this for him. Make it all okay. That little girl blends into the adult woman who has compassion for a person looking at the slow and unpredictable approach of his own death. I *want* to make it all okay for him, as I wanted to do for all those for whom I was chaplain.

If I were his chaplain, not his daughter, I think it would be possible to just listen. To help him find the bread among the stones for himself. But for Dad, I can't seem to muster that detachment. So, I must settle for soothing, which is at least better than arguing. I hope. But not any more effective. I think he actually needs to mourn. We probably need to mourn together, but I am so afraid of his pain. Just as he is afraid of it; his pain is deep and old.

And so I say the next morning, hoping to reopen the conversation: "When you feel so blue, you could consider where you are today, right now—you have family who love you, I and your grandson and your step-grandsons have meaningful work, we have loving partners, we are happy people, and you had a hand in making us as we are. You have great-grand-children who are filled with joy and life, and you have a hand in that, too. Nieces and nephews, your sister . . ." Stones to bread, how jolly . . .

He nods, obediently smiles. I know he treasures all of that, but I also know it is not enough. I can't make him a happy person who counts his blessings any more than I, as a chaplain, could take away the fear of a father whose adult son was dying without "being saved." Or the fears of parents who believed that permitting a blood transfusion for their desperately ill child would condemn that child to hell. Or of a terrified patient who be-lieved the devil was causing her cancer. With all of those I could overlook (or at least grit my teeth at) the "bad theology," yet find a way to journey along, and lift up whatever I heard in their words of hope or faith or trust—in God's love, in human commitment, in the future, in the doctor, in what-ever was going to get that person through one more day. My father is not using theological language, yet his reality is as grim as anyone who believes we are all "sinners in the hands of an angry God."[5]

***

Dad and I had a skirmish last night, occasioned by my wanting to remove a wilted dahlia covered with aphids from a bouquet. He strongly objected, I got mad internally and then snappish with him. Somehow that became a conversation about his opinion that he doesn't "need a babysitter," mean-ing, "No caregivers here when you go away!" "I can't afford it!" And so on. Then I remembered that he'd had to pay two big bills that afternoon, which always triggers anxiety for him. Our fight about the dahlia, which I had immediately interpreted as being my fault, was actually a fight he started in his generalized anxiety state as a distraction.

Noticing that kind of thing is very difficult for me, accustomed as I am to always feeling like the guilty party around my dad, but Allen (who, of course, is biased in my favor, so I discount what he says somewhat, rightly or wrongly) felt that it was quite obvious that my father was picking a fight.

---

5. Edwards, "Sinners in the Hands."

Once I got the idea that my dad was anxious about money, we had an edgy, irritable conversation about that. He's right that it's his money, his body, his health. I'm right that it wouldn't be responsible to leave him here alone for hours. Right? Am I right? I think so.

Buried in this conversation about money is my fear of his neediness. I am sure that what he really means is, "*You* can do whatever I need, and if you won't, then I'll manage alone." He is so intricate in his lack of self-knowledge and I am so well-trained in my sense of obligation to providing his happiness that we never get this sorted out. I angrily tell him that I can't do everything, and I can't ask Allen to do everything, and he says again, "I can manage alone," and then I say, "No, you can't," and remind him of the time he spilled his water and then fell while walking in it; his general unsteadiness; the need for shopping and housework and errands; and then he feels defensive and afraid, and then I feel guilty, and then we both get more and more annoyed . . .

Dad is more worried about his money running out than he is about being alone. He insists that I shouldn't plan my life around him, that I should get another full-time job. He denies his frailty. And I am in the shame-inducing place of wanting to make him admit that he is old and weak and has lost some of his abilities and needs me and what I provide and the people whose help I enlist. Shame inducing for me, because I feel like I "should" feel more compassion for him and just let all this go in one ear and out the other. I want him to be honest with himself and with me that this is the end of his life, goddamn it. But I stop short of saying that, always, of course.

He says, "I need my money for a rainy day."

And I say, "Dad, this is a rainy day. It's raining."

The place we are in is not unique, I hear versions of this in other families' stories.

My inner voice pleads: *Oh, please, please, universe, when I am truly old or frail, let me understand what is happening to me. Let me accept it, and make it easier for my family by so doing. Let there be conversations that can encompass, briefly or at length, the love, the history, the sorrow of farewell, the mystery and the meaning.*

Last night I was able to be gentle with him once I understood what we were talking about. I tried to turn the conversation to what he might want to say about how he wants to live out his final years. (Months? Days?) But he wouldn't go there. He referred to something my Great-Aunt Alice wrote on the wall of the cabin in the format of an addition problem: "Save" on one line, "More" underneath it, then the line that indicates "equals," and under that, "Money." He was half smiling when he quoted this to me as a joke, but I couldn't go there to the place where we laugh about the Hildebrand anxiety about money.

Instead, I said, "Do you really want that to be the philosophy that rules this part of your life?" It's too real to laugh about. And actually, as much as I wish I could have a bird's-eye view of this time, of these struggles between him and me, as much as I wish I could rise above the fury that our interactions elicit in me so often, I am also really, really sick of this. Not sick of it because I have been doing it for three months. Sick of it because I have been doing it for my entire life. Trying to make him happy. Trying to get him to affirm me and be open about the love that I do believe he feels for me. And then just giving up. Until the next time.

3

The Netherworld of Loss

WHAT HAVE THEY GIVEN me—those years spent as a chaplain in the netherworld of loss? Thankfully, I have not had losses of my own, but there is a different kind of trauma from time spent with all those parents whose baby, whose child, whose teenager was dead. Or dying. Or chronically ill. Or dying after years of being chronically ill.

What has it given me to be with the medical staff who cared for those babies, those children, those teenagers, sometimes for many admissions, for the years of their careers? Their work was interleaved with the work of caring for children who had less serious things wrong and got well, unlike the chaplain's work. Folks for whom there are happy outcomes don't usually want to talk with the chaplain. The medical staff had the most intimate kind of relationships with these little patients; they took care of their bodies throughout nights of pain and sleepless fretfulness, vomiting, tears, and loneliness.

One gift from those years: my perception of life's purpose is different from what it once was, that's for sure. People say of the deaths of children that this is an upset of the natural order, that parents are supposed to die first. But children and babies die all the time. Some of these deaths are preventable, as in girl babies killed at birth because of their gender. Or babies starving to death or bombed or beaten. Not all are, though. We are mammals, and mammals sometimes have genes that go awry. Mammals have bodies that get illnesses, that get injured. Stuff happens.

The Netherworld of Loss

The baby who is miscarried. The baby who is stillborn at thirty-nine weeks, or dies during delivery. The baby whose cancer shows up at six months of age. The baby born with any of a number of heart defects, mitochondrial defects, brain defects, or gut defects. What is the purpose of that? The purpose for the parents, for the baby herself? But why does there even have to be a purpose? Western civilization, with its heavy influence on history as a linear narrative—beginning, middle, end, all imbued with *meaning*—in Judaism and Christianity and Islam, insists that we look for this. Our concept of purpose is a gift from the "religions of the Book." Although from what little I know about religions other than my own, I think this need for there to be purpose is actually everywhere. Hard-wired in human beings. Which is, of course, likely why that idea turned up in theology in the first place.

But it is hard to see meaning and purpose in the suffering of babies and children, and particularly in their deaths. I reject, I have to reject, the idea that children's suffering and dying young are "God's will." Grieving adults will do their best to make meaning of heart-rending loss in some fashion and that is the convenient catchall—sometimes with anger and alienation, other times with resignation and acceptance. I once asked a Somali Muslim nurse friend what a support group for Somali Muslim mothers who have lost pregnancies could look like, since none of those moms came to the groups we had for parents who had experienced a fetal demise. She said, "You couldn't have a group like that. No one would come, because if you did, someone would be sure to say to the mother, you are not accepting God's will. You are going against God."

I, with my liberal Protestant theology, reject that! I reject the idea that we cannot question God's will, God's actions, God's purposes. But what do I know about what it takes to survive loss as a Somali Muslim refugee woman? I never tried to offer purpose, meaning, to parents or grandparents or aunts and uncles and cousins and friends or the staff. But I never contradicted their meaning-making either. I just spent time with them—as much time as they wanted and as I could offer. Just being with them. Leave the meaning-making aside and focus on presence and relationship.

On the days when I was also on call for the adult hospital, where families were losing adult loved ones or where the dying person was awake, articulate, and aware of their own impeding death—none of that was easy either. Their deaths were more like my own will most likely be. And although some were eager to be out of pain, no one I ever talked with was eager to die, except those who had tried to kill themselves. But even they, unexpectedly alive after almost dying, were mostly glad to find themselves still on Planet Earth.

I didn't meet many people who were ready to say goodbye forever. Most people want at least one more sunrise or sunset or snowstorm or tulip or something. Contemplating the magnitude of the dead, Lafcadio Hearn's "vast Amazon,"[1] doesn't really comfort anyone, either. We know that we all go there, but we don't go there together. We all know that we die alone.

Now I am walking with my father to his death, just as surely as escorting him to an executioner's block. We both assume that his death will come before mine, although who knows, really? It's like walking in a gathering snowstorm, in winter dusk, out onto a partially frozen lake. The ice *will* break but when? I'll have to let go of his hand, the weight of the breaking will pull him under, away from me, he *will* vanish into the icy water. Even if I died with him, we would each die alone. I think. No way to know, of course, what happens when we reach the biological end point of our own time.

Maybe those years of pediatric chaplaincy make it possible for me to feel the luxury of this October day, in spite of everything. The sand running out in my own hourglass before I have accomplished much with this life, half of which so far I spent wading deeply into alcoholism, drug addiction, the aftereffects of growing up in a dysfunctional family, and half of which, so far, I have spent wading out. I drop into sleep at night with the cares of the day falling off of me as easily as petals from a flower. I wake with the same easiness, like a flower opening to light. None of the drivenness of my time at the hospital. Little of the anger that hounded me last summer when this part of my life with my dad began. I have located myself in the netherworld, now on my own behalf.

***

A gray morning. In this autumn season where we have had one brutally brilliant day after another, in drought, days in which the sun felt dangerous and hostile despite the beauty of light on red blueberry barrens. Exhausted zinnias still blooming in late October, tomatoes that started to bear in July still putting forth fruit. You can almost hear the trees longing for water, the rain that doesn't come. The fires in California burn on, despite days of firefighting. Puerto Rico and many of the Caribbean islands are without

---

1. Hearn, "Dust," 642.

clean drinking water, electricity, shelter, or food after three hurricanes in a row in September. The president in this country is an ignorant and bigoted buffoon, racist, sexist, homophobic, and wields great power with the support, still, of much of the Republican leadership in Washington and his "base." My mother would have been enraged. My father wants so much to outlive this administration. I feel the wonderment of my father's slow passing, while California turns to ash, and the southeast United States and the Caribbean strangle in mud. Here there are sugar maples on the hillside behind our house, the flame of their leaves hidden amongst dark spruce. And lichens gray as smoke. Everything so precious, so vulnerable.

I am actually wandering in a gray morning day after day now, a gray morning all my own. A few of my friendships seem to have died in this time—not on the other person's side but on mine. Relationships that I felt sustained by have suddenly been revealed to be inconsequential, lacking in the firm fiber that won't break under stress. I open up my hands and these relationships drop away. I let them go, intent on understanding myself and on the narrowing focus of my family life. Was it that these people have been stand-ins, relationships where I got triggered or affirmed and worked internally on the residue from my messed-up childhood family, and now I am doing that internal work directly stimulated by being with my dad so much? Were these friendships just manifestations of my codependence? Years-long manifestations, relationships that I didn't even recognize as ones that couldn't meet my needs?

As I sidle up to death—my father's approaching; my mother's twenty years ago but still fresh; my own, my husband's, my best friend's, my cat's—who knows, who knows, which death, which time—I feel no more prepared than when I was younger and only thought about it all with bravado. But there is a reason why I chose to work with the dying and why I choose to think so much about these things. I want to be located, in history, on the planet, in time and space, and in myself. I don't want to drift. I want to make a narrative.

Terrible, massive fires still burn out west. Last night at suppertime for me, Dad, and Allen, here in coastal Maine, after another very gray day, unusual this dry year, there was a sudden band of light on the garden on the west side of the house, so brilliant and unexpected that I first thought it was some sort of human-made phenomenon. But I couldn't imagine why there would be a searchlight over our shaggy lawn and ragged fields and garden. When I went outside to look, I found myself in the midst of a fiery sunset, orange light over everything that had been gray and dim, igniting it. And on the ridge behind the house, the poplar leaves shimmering in the whisper of the end-of-day breeze looked just like flames. Ephemeral as the sun sank behind the trees to the west. The look of kindled coals lay on the trees to the east. Ephemeral, achingly beautiful, fearsome in what these flames of sunset resembled.

***

Back in the inner dark place again. The very dark place. Allen is about to be gone for a week again, and it will be extremely hard to have him away. Hard physically as there will be no one to share the slowly increasing dad-chores with, but even harder emotionally, as there will be no buffer between me and Dad.

The pattern seems to go like this: I am with Dad, sitting beside him at the kitchen table as our day together begins, trying to make pleasant conversation. To build a connection. He can't hear me so I have to speak loudly and clearly and he still can't hear me, which begins to frustrate me, because his not hearing seems so intermittent that it is hard not to feel he is doing it on purpose. So reminiscent of the years and years of his "selective hearing" or inattention, when it just seemed like it was everybody else's job to make sure he heard. Maybe he was gradually getting deaf, even in his forties. But it seemed then, and seems now, hostile.

Assuming I persist and we engage, then the conversation—which I, for some reason having to do with my own denial and minimization, always think is going to include finding some common ground, but usually does not—feels like a power struggle. He wants me to wring my hands and bemoan the cloudy sky: "It will rain on the kids' soccer game; the game will be cancelled." (Is this really code for "I don't want you to go to the soccer game"?)

He wants me to be interested in the fact that he heard on the news some new data bit about how awful our president is. Some data bit that I have heard several times already and which I am heartily sick of hearing. It is not revelatory; it is tawdry and horrifying. It is the news cycle which needs to endlessly go, "My, my, my!" about the same stuff instead of the journalists actually going out and finding new stories, some of which might be just information and some of which might even be encouraging. Life is not all about a president and his minions. Even more, this endless babbling about how bad the world is and how much worse it could be doesn't seem to inspire anyone with power to actually *do* anything different and new.

Dad wants me to worry with him, to be upset with him. And I resist. Not by quietly listening, but by listening with growing irritation for a while and then pushing his anxiety loop away from me—being brusque, being hearty—"Rain? No, it will only be a little cloudy! And they would never cancel a game!"

By this time, we are really in the weeds, in the jungle. He is blundering along verbally with facial expressions that show how annoyed he is, which irritates me more. I am also blundering along, feeling more and more pissed off. The plan I had at the beginning of the day about creating a nice calm connection with him is out the window. I don't want to even bring him his orange juice, I want to go back upstairs and brood. But the feelings, the feelings. Equal parts anger at him and guilt that I am a bad daughter. That once again I have proved myself to be irritable, unstable, mean-spirited, and the Problem.

How did I go from being "Wudge" or "Kitten" as a little girl to being a constant irritation to him by the time I went to junior high school? Was it that, by then, my mother had introduced me to drinking and I was choosing to emulate her stubborn, nonconformist ways? How can I, at this late date and after all sorts of therapy, feel that he has failed me as a father and yet also believe that the real problem is that I have failed him as a daughter?

***

Several years ago, when I was a parish minister in a rural Maine church, I had the opportunity to observe the creation of, and subsequent dismantling of, a sand mandala made by Venerable Lama Losang Samten, a Tibetan Buddhist scholar and former monk who visited our community at the invitation of a local crafts school. The mandala was of the Wheel of Life, and the individual images illustrated the stages of human existence, with its trials and temptations, griefs and joys, and the human passage from birth to death. These images drawn in sand remind the viewer of life's impermanence—the fleeting evanescence of all we experience, all we treasure, of the meaningful and wonderful lives we create, in their rich variety of form and shape and color—lives made of sand.

Using the simplest of tools—two long, thin cones with ridges on them, and pots of differently colored sand—Losang created people and animals, gods and demigods, houses, boats, and temples in minute and exact detail.

With a firm hand and great patience, Losang spent the better part of seven days making this mandala out of tiny grains of carefully placed sand, and all who came to watch were invited to be present at the dismantling ceremony on the afternoon of the last day. He was asked many questions about how he had learned to do the work of mandala-making, about how he learned the traditional forms of the mandalas he made, and at the same time, learned how to improvise and adjust them to the different settings in which he created them. Years of rigorous training and practice go into learning the craft; hours and hours go into the making of a mandala. When one awestruck visitor commented on the patience and the concentration required, Losang nodded quietly. And then, when the same visitor asked in a hushed voice how long it would take to dismantle the week's work, Losang grinned and snapped his fingers. "No time at all! Like that!" he said.

The room was full for the dismantling ceremony, which began with chanting and prayers; the crowd watched in silence as Losang moved around the table, pinching up certain of the tiny images made of sand. He cut through the exquisite design with one of the metal tools he had used to create the mandala, slicing it up boldly. And lastly, he took a disposable foam-rubber paint brush, the kind you buy at the hardware store—a dozen for ten dollars—and swept the colored sand in long strokes toward the center of the table. Tiny green trees laden with fruit; little pink and yellow people; an orange lobster, a white pig; tiered buildings of red, white, and gold; snow-capped mountains; a miniature of the local church where I was pastor—all the colors of the rainbow, piled together in a soft gray heap. A heap that looked like ashes.

And I thought, that is just like what is left at the end of our lives. We spend years making the work of art that is our life—and it is just like a sand painting, impermanent by design. Impermanence, limitation, death—part of God's good and beloved creation. Each life has beautiful images, rich colors, complicated patterns, and it is God's purpose for each of us that we live as fully as we can, that we make our lives intricate and detailed, but at the end, all we have done and all that we are is swept away, like a small pile of ashes. Which is also God's purpose.

Jesus says of the rich man with his barns full of goods, "You fool! This very night your life is being demanded of you. And the things you have prepared, whose will they be? So it is with those who store up treasures for themselves but are not rich toward God."[2] How harsh this seems! Yet, if we

---

2. Luke 12:20b–21.

can really listen to these words, we will hear a liberating truth: life is not meant to be acquisition and worry. Life is meant to be communion with God—with what is eternal, rather than with what is always fading away, getting lost, subject to rot and ruin and theft. It is God's good gift that we enjoy our lives; and Jesus points out that the only firm foundation for our joy in living is God. Make the picture of your life beautiful, even while you know that it is made of sand.

4

Deeper into the Labyrinth

Now that my dad has been stable for a few weeks, now that I am used to the rhythm of his care and his needs, now that I have some distance from the loss I felt when I left my hospital job to come home and care for him, now that three more months of my own therapy have passed, I find myself in the null place of grief. Not the new grief that anyone might feel when walking toward death with an aging parent, but my lifelong grief. The grief that addiction always covered for me. I am just sort of floating in it.

I want to eat a lot of rich, flavorful food. Salty, buttery, sweet. Various textures. To eat endlessly; but when I think about it, I can't really imagine which food would do it for me. No food would. I guess what is different in this from my overeating past is that I know that the answer to my feelings of sadness and aimlessness is not food. Nor is it in the physical act of getting the food into my mouth as fast as possible, to get the sensation of a full stomach and fill in the empty spaces of my middle. My middle is empty for other reasons. I can handle the emptiness if I stay aware of it and get support and am self-nurturing. All that boring stuff. But of course, that is stuff that works, that got me off of addictive eating years ago, and also helped me be done with alcohol and drugs and obsessive relationships.

I want the thrill of flirting, of new discoveries of someone else's brain, emotions, some blank slate (never really blank) on which I can write my ideas and my program for that other person's happiness and well-being. Instead of my own. I want intense intellectual engagement, affirming feedback, all tinged with a touch of sexuality. But like the food, I don't really want that. I don't want it because it is nothingness, it is vapor, it is illusion. I have real relationships, vastly more meaningful and important to me than a collection of new people could ever be. Like the food, there is really no way to find the right flavor, texture, quantity, combination. It doesn't exist.

I want to travel with my husband, I want to see new places, to eat out, go to the movies. I want to be in motion, perpetually, so that I can stay ahead of my thoughts. Also ahead of my feelings, or the absence of my feelings. Ahead of the blankness. Which brings me back to grief. I have learned, slowly and clumsily, thanks to my therapist and a lot of hard work, thanks to self-help books and twelve-step programs, that fundamentally and most of all, what I have to do and maybe what anyone has to do, unless they were blessed with a "happy enough" childhood, is grieve. That honest grieving is the first step into accepting life as it is . . .

Dry. The air is so dry. The sunlight has a hostile feel to it, too bright for our trees and fields and water, like the light of the desert. One day after another of clear blue sky, and warm breezes. But this is New England, this is Maine, this is late autumn. There's supposed to be a bite to the air by now. There's supposed to have been a killing frost. The flowers are going by, running out of energy with which to bloom, but the plants are still green, confused, trying.

My dad has gone deeper into the labyrinth of his ending. He is much more forgetful, and less aware that he has forgotten things. He just asks for the same information over and over—without accusing me of having withheld it, thankfully. We changed one medication, and now he takes a pill a half hour after supper instead of at bedtime. Every evening he asks, "Why am I taking this pill now?" Every morning after his one pre-breakfast pill and his vitamins, he asks, "Will I take any other pills today?"

He watches *NewsHour* on PBS only because he has always watched *NewsHour*, I think. And he can still make very astute comments about world events, political personalities, and the interplay of history with the present moment. But it is clear that his favorite stories on the program are the ones about the arts and the ones that tell people's ordinary/extraordinary stories. He doesn't want to think about the state of the world the way he once did. The world he is leaving, in stages. He smiles more than he did last summer. I think he feels better physically than he did for several months after the pneumonia, when he was terribly weak. And maybe he has lost just enough mental acuity to be less anxious for the first time in his life.

I have gone deeper into the labyrinth of life's ending with him. As we travel together, I want there to be space inside of me and around me so I can let this vast experience of letting go of him be as large as it needs to be. I don't want to be clawing at the surface of it. It has taken me a long time to get here, this place where I don't want to keep my dad at arm's length. There is a boundary between us now, made partially by his reduced articulation of his abiding anxiety, but also by my greater ability to stay apart from it. As I am more able to stand apart from him, I am able to feel more affection and patience.

I feel tenderness toward him now. Not every moment. But often. The young man he was, the life he lived. The things that damaged him. The way he prevailed anyway.

The apostle Paul says, "But we have this treasure in clay jars."[1] Paul is speaking of the contrast between our power and God's. We could say that the treasure is the gift of life itself. We are very frail, we are breakable. We hold the treasure of our humanity, all that is best and brightest about us, within the most fragile of vessels, our limitations and weaknesses. And what Paul says about this, our human condition, is that God is with us. God knows how we are made, full of contradictions and calamities, and comes to join us in our lives, comes to be one with us, over and over again, just as we are.

***

Yesterday we finally met with a caregiver agency. A very nice young man came all the way from Bangor to meet us, and what he had to say about services and availability and schedule sounded fine. The price was what I expected, twenty-four dollars per hour. My dad was not enthusiastic about even meeting with the guy and the money clearly freaked him out. But he is different from last summer: less rigid and demanding of me, more accepting of his limitations. I think for both of us this is perhaps a calm time in between the debilitating blow of the pneumonia last June, the slow recovery from it, and whatever comes next.

I'm still hoping for Dad to have a nice quiet death in his sleep before there is another blow. And hoping that he doesn't live for ten more years, so that Allen and I can have freedom to enjoy our own "young old age." But for right now, hiring a regularly scheduled caregiver doesn't feel right. The money feels out of reach. I feel peaceful about the decision not to hire

---

1. 2 Cor 4:7a.

a companion yet. It feels as if incorporating another personality into our household and its routines would take more than it would give. We are still getting used to a new cat! Who seems to be very bonded to me, but merely tolerant of my dad and Allen. I think we have all accepted that she is *my* cat, even though she was meant to be a shared cat. She has her own ideas.

And at last, it is raining. It rained in that tantalizing "almost" way yesterday, but truly settled into a real, steady rainfall last night and is still raining this morning. Though the weather is weirdly warm for the end of October, at least it is raining. The grass and much of the underbrush is springtime green and looks shockingly vibrant against the yellows, reds, and browns of the trees. The landscape has slowly altered as some leaves drop and some branches become bare, as the asters and goldenrod finally go to seed. Even while the temperature of the air is like early autumn, true autumn has come.

Like my dad's decline. This is not precipitous, not what one would expect for a nearly ninety-eight-year-old. But he's living in a different season, nonetheless.

5

Detach Over and Over

THE UNDERLYING SADNESS THAT I feel these days doesn't go away, although it changes. Last summer, when the caregiving began, the sadness was blunt and raw; now it is more subtle and pervasive. Last summer, it was overpowering and I couldn't name it, couldn't detail it, couldn't figure out what was past and what was present. What came from leaving my beloved job and what came from being at my dad's house? That's all clearer now: leaving my job was a loss I am moving beyond and learning from as I continue my life; being at my dad's house means integrating the loss of him into a much, much deeper understanding of mortality as we say slow goodbyes and as my own death draws closer.

My dad is dying, and my husband and I also are, of course, like all people, all of us on unknown trajectories toward our own endings. I do the daily tasks of my dad's care, still not greatly time-consuming, but slightly more so as days pass into weeks and months. His hearing aids in and out, his bed made, his commode emptied, his breakfast, lunch, and dinner prepared. All small and ordinary, nothing like changing diapers or repositioning a body that has lost self-control, although by the time we get to that, if we get to that, he will probably be a hospice patient or in a nursing home, so we would have help that the healthcare system doesn't offer us now, and maybe that would make it easier.

Since Dad has no diagnosis, he doesn't get any services paid for by Medicare or his insurance. But I can't bathe him, can't wash his hair or clip

Detach Over and Over

his toenails without my husband's help and my father's agreement, and he won't agree unless he has energy and when he has energy, my husband and I aren't always both present here at home, so weeks go by without basic tasks of hygiene. Ridiculous. Fortunately for us, the way hospice care is set up in our rural area means that there is a separate agency which provides volunteers for patients, and their admission standards are more lenient than formal Medicare hospice standards are. My dad has qualified for volunteer support before he has qualified for medical support, and has a wonderful relationship with a man who comes weekly and talks about everything from a wild grouse he is taming to my dad's memories of service in World War II. That hour or so a week means a break for me and Allen, and also means that my dad, reduced though he is, has the capacity to make a new friend.

I am doing all this caregiving work for someone who almost never expresses any joy or gratitude or love. However, I can't require that my dad take pleasure in his life for my sake. It is my job to detach, to detach over and over again from his negativity, his mistrust.

That is one aspect of his behavior that is so difficult, that in spite of everything, in spite of all that we do for him, he panics when he suddenly thinks that the house is empty, that he has been left here alone. How can he think that, it enrages me. I know intellectually that it is from the uncertainties in his past, combined with his present-day feeling of vulnerability. But it is part of what makes me feel that he does not take in the actual parameters of this time, and therefore, all that I am and all that I do is unappreciated. Allen and I have rearranged our priorities and given up things that are important to us just so he won't be at home alone. If we have to go to the store, the post office, or an appointment, we tell him, we reassure him, and we sometimes hire someone to be here with him. Yet he acts like it is legitimate for him to expect that he has been abandoned. And I recognize the helplessness he feels, the fears of what each moment could bring, but, shamefully, I still get offended.

I know, somewhere in my heart of hearts, that it *is* legitimate for him to fear abandonment, to expect it even; not because it will happen now, but because it happened long ago and he never recovered. What little I know about the emotional world of his childhood sounds pretty grim. It's not my job to fix all that, although I have tried. Tried because my mother and my father acted like it *was* indeed my job, to make my father happy. But I can't fix it. If only I could get to the heart of my own lack and my own loss—whatever it is that drives *me* to immature fears and baseless worries.

Because then maybe I could be more patient with my father and my husband and expect less of the world. Give more, take less, be at peace.

Yesterday I picked up the small bouquet I had made a few days before to add more water to it, and he said, angrily, "Don't throw that away!" I got pissed off. Feeling red hot instantly, I snapped, "Don't micromanage me!" Then I added water and put the flowers back on the table by his place. I felt ashamed for snapping. Felt resentful. I added those emotions to the percolating brew of failure that I feel.

As I thought about the interaction later, I remembered that since last summer when I started putting little bouquets by his place at the table because he doesn't have the mobility to go outside and look at the garden anymore, we have had this contretemps more than once. I pick off a dead bloom or finally decide that the whole bouquet is tired and faded, and he wants it left untouched, in place: brown leaves, stinking water, blackening flower heads and all. Untouched like so much that is in this house, flyspecked and covered with greasy dust. But for God's sake, I am struggling with my father yet again over a few marigolds and calendulas in a jar.

And so, I am sad, sad because I am so constantly engaged in an ancient power struggle with my dad. It takes so much energy to do the tasks and feel the feelings of this.

Is there anyone, anywhere who knows what I am feeling? This particular mix of necessary physical care with possibly unnecessary, certainly disproportionate codependent emotional care...

I wrote those last few sentences with full awareness that, yes, there is someone (in fact, there are many someones) who knows exactly what I am going through. My dynamic with my father is as common as dirt. It poses an interesting combination of challenges, being an only child in my particular family, with an alcoholic mother and an anxiety-ridden dad, in the suburbs, in the fifties; a family not financially able to keep up with the Joneses, and actually scorning them, and without fitting in in many ways. But the challenges are not unique. And I am hoping to forgive my father, and even more importantly to deeply, truly, wholly forgive myself, before he dies. Before I die.

***

During my years of commuting to my chaplain's job, I had three hours driving on Friday afternoons and on Sunday afternoons to think a lot about the place of religion in general, and Christianity in particular, in the modern

United States of America. Many, many of the young parents I spent time with while they were at the hospital for the crisis of their child's illness or injury were not part of faith communities. Many had had negative experiences with religion. But they were desperate for something to hold on to, and I tried to be that something for people of "no religious preference" and atheists, as well as for those who were part of faith communities, whether they were Jewish, Muslim, Buddhist, Hindu, or Christian. Many of these people had a lot of painful ideas—like that God had given their child cancer because they, the parent, had stopped going to church, or drank too much, or had had an affair. And while I did my best to offer these parents alternative ideas, I had to admit that many faith communities have, indeed, taught that sort of thing. And still do.

    I don't know how people put together meaning and purpose, or where they find hope and courage, unless they tell me. But my experiences as a parish minister and as a chaplain make me believe that the concerns of people who have no interest in religion or have negative feelings about it are, in truth, much the same as the concerns of religious people: health, happiness, family, friends, love, peace, and making a positive difference in the world.

* * *

Yesterday was a very hard day. Dad could not understand the process by which he had renewed his subscription to *The New Yorker*. The whole business of paying for things online has been hard for him many times, usually because he doesn't complete the forms thoroughly and fails to click the final box, and so he ends up not performing the task he thinks he is performing. But this event was different. He and I had filled out the form together to renew the subscription and he subsequently received an acknowledgment email. I thought we were all set after several months of fretting about this. But evidently, at some prior point he had done the renewal process by himself online but not actually paid, so, suddenly, here was a bill for a subscription, which upset him enormously. I was puzzled at first, until it dawned on me what must have happened. Allen called *The New Yorker* and clarified that we only wanted one subscription, they cancelled the extra one with no hassle, and we were all set once again.

    But then Dad's credit card bill for the past month arrived and there was the charge for the *New Yorker* subscription, and he was furious. "What a racket! Why won't they leave me alone? I thought Allen fixed this. Why am I being billed?"

No matter how I explained it, no matter what I said, he could not get the idea that, yes, the subscription he and I had filled out online was all set, and *The New Yorker* had been paid by his credit card company. He couldn't grasp that the charge on the bill in his hands only meant that he now had to pay the credit card company. He got madder and madder at me, began to question all the charges on the bill, said he couldn't afford to pay it at all, *wouldn't* pay it. Somewhere in all of this, he grabbed the cat from where she had seated herself on the arm of his chair, hoping for a treat, and tried to make her sit on his lap, saying, "If you want to be a friend, then you can have a treat. Otherwise, forget it!"

The cat struggled out of his grasp and hasn't been near him since, not even when he shakes the jar of treats at her.

Finally, Dad told me, in a very sarcastic tone, that he'd had enough of my lecturing him for one day, which pushed my buttons for sure. I was barely keeping it together anyway as he had been accusatory and sarcastic to varying degrees throughout my forty-five minutes of trying to talk him down and help him see what the process of renewing his subscription entailed. So, I got pissed off too, and equally sarcastically said, "Thank you, Alice, for trying so hard to help me understand this." Then I went upstairs where I stayed, with my book, while he watched television downstairs.

Fortunately, his sister came for a visit and he had a distraction. Allen and I and the cat took a nap. I knew during the whole episode that the likelihood was that he really could not grasp what was going on, and also that he knew that he couldn't, and that this was scaring him. I knew that many, if not most, people who are losing some of their mental acuity get hostile and paranoid. But knowing that didn't help, partly because this is old territory. It's not as though he had been a trusting, collaborative, open partner with me before and now is changing. That would be a different kind of heartbreak. This anxious person, continually on the lookout for an attack, is who he has often been. He hasn't gotten to the point where Allen and I have to wrest control of anything from him, which would be horrible, and I hope that doesn't happen. Dad's end of life seems more like it will be slow diminishment, gradual ebbing. I guess I know that there is no new, unique skill set required for me to learn to respond to his negativity. It's just the same old skill set that I've been slowly learning and practicing for a long time. Boundaries. Setting psychic and emotional limits. Detachment, hopefully with love.

Detach Over and Over

***

And now, this morning, the moment we have all been waiting for (said sarcastically): Dad has a cold. Learning this, immediately I felt guilty—guilty for all the times when I wanted him to get pneumonia again and this time, quietly, peacefully die. Or preferably, since I am not an ogre and have no need for revenge, I wanted him to die *before* he gets pneumonia again, since I don't want him to suffer, to be in pain or frightened, but just to go. His death will release me to live my own life and flounder along in my own dilemmas.

I know that this life will eventually end—mine, as well as his, of course—and I also can't believe that it will ever end. But Dad has a cold and this could mean something. Something is changing. Maybe.

Something could get better.

Something could get worse.

I love my dad. I don't want him to be sick or to suffer. And, I want to be free. We often get along better when he is sick. Some of that is surely me feeling tender and protective—but maybe also guilty and scared? Some of that is him, too, it occurred to me today. He is less intense and more grateful when he is sick.

I don't know, I can't figure it out. I am so tired of this, and it still may just be the beginning. I feel as though I have sleepwalked through too much of my life, years of substance abuse, years of anxiety. But I am so fortunate, so blessed to have the cabin as a place of retreat and grounding. A place I went limping back to so many times, after so many defeats, from the world outside of me or generated by the world within. A place I could mark out the dimensions of, and measure myself against. I know this one small place so intimately and yet there is so much there I do not know at all. The secret lives of the eiders, for whom the wintry shores of Blue Hill Bay are warmer and more fecund than the Arctic where they summer. The gulls, unconcerned when the sky is gray, or the wind is lashing up whitecaps. All the animals who wait for nighttime to find their food, seeking to eat and not be eaten. The blueberry and alder and wild rose which stubbornly, persistently come up in the lawn in between mowings. The wildflowers in any corner of a field that isn't mowed. And dawn over Cadillac Mountain, or sunset at the top of the rise to the west of the cabin. The Milky Way covering a wide swath of sky at night. Fitting myself into the web of it, feeling accompanied by the tides, by daybreak and moonrise. While it remains a mystery to me, and I remain a mystery to myself.

A Matter of Death and Life

***

One springtime evening during the nine-year period when we lived full time in the cabin, Allen and I took a quiet row out to a seal rookery, a small island of rocks and sand that sits far out in the bay. I wanted to get away from the ongoing bad news of a devastating oil spill in the Gulf of Mexico and see the pristine natural world. I wanted to see the baby seals, something I'd been hoping to do since the time a few years ago when Allen and his eldest son came back from a row to that island and described seeing the pups and their mothers all around the boat. We'd been hearing the seals every night—barking, squealing, chirping, harrumphing—long after the seagulls had gone to bed, although the seals can be so noisy that the gulls rouse and half-heartedly join the ruckus, sounding not quite as efficient and on top of things as they usually do. The seals sound like a loving family with a lot to say to each other who all talk at once!

We slowly rowed along the rocky bar that stretches out from the mainland, and as we got further off shore, we began to see seals hauled out on the ledges—and they started calling out and flumping down into the water to swim near our boat. Soon we had an escort of ten or so large seals, who seemed calmly curious about us. As we got closer to their island nursery, the mothers there decided to get in the water too, and we could see what looked like the very beach itself in motion, in waves of rockweed color and granite color as seal mothers and pups gathered themselves up and headed into the sea. All very wonderful and just what I'd been hoping to see.

It never occurred to me that my pleasure was at the seals' expense. But after the fact, in order to better understand what I had seen, I did some online research about harbor seals and their habits. And then I learned that the cute behaviors of the cute seals—increased vocalizing; seals at rest raising their heads to watch us; hauled-out seals returning to the water—are all signs that the seals are upset. Are all signs that we were too close, even though we were about two hundred feet away.

As we drew near to the seals' island, I noticed an eagle perched on the high point of a rock overlooking the beach. The eagle was more obviously cautious about us than the seals were—he flew off when we were still quite far away. I worried about why an eagle was hanging out on an island with a lot of baby seals . . . And just as I had easily assumed that the seals were curious and friendly rather than disturbed, I assumed that the eagle had been attacking the pups, and I was glad that our approach had scared him off. The seals were good, the eagle was bad—even though I could tell myself

Detach Over and Over

that it's all part of the balance of nature, that the eagle and the eagle's young have to eat, too—but seals are more emotionally accessible, somehow . . .

I was upset by what I thought of as the eagle's threat to the seals and completely unaware of my own impact on them. My subsequent research told me that eagles eat from seal carcasses, not from live seals. Eagles hang around seal birthings to clean up placentas and pups born dead—a pretty good way to keep the beaches clean and safe for the living. Mostly eagles eat fish, but, as eagle populations recover from a near wipeout caused by DDT, they are finding that there aren't as many fish as there once were, and scientists are concerned that eagles may be poisoned all over again as they seek other sources of food and eat the DDT-laced fat of seal carcasses. When I thought back on the event, I recognized that the approach of our rowboat was more distressing to the seals than the eagle perched above their beach was, since they lay around relaxing despite his presence. And of course, a tide of petroleum spilled by humans and DDT still permeating their environment is far more dangerous to both of them than they would ever be to each other.

In Genesis we read that we have been given "dominion"[1] over the works of God's hands and we Christians have latched firmly onto that idea. We are the bosses of the natural world! Once upon a time we were puny and frail but could reason and plan in ways vastly more sophisticated than the animals around us, and now our technologies make us mighty indeed. We do have dominion—defined as supreme authority and control—over the works of God's hands. We are the bosses—and yet, we really don't know much about what goes on in the natural world. The subtle interplay of all the parts of creation is something we are slowly beginning to understand—and even folks with extensive education and training can entirely misconstrue what they observe, even in fellow humans, let alone in other species. Far too often we are exercisers of an unfortunate kind of dominion—an absolute power that operates in ignorance. Even folks with the best intentions, all the good will in the world, folks who don't like to use the word "dominion" but prefer "stewardship" with its connotations of responsibility and care, can do great harm to the natural world. And by so doing, great harm to themselves and their children and their children's children.

The seal and the eagle have coexisted for millennia. They are not problems to each other, out there on the rocky, barren islands. Allen and I, not out to hunt or build shelter or compete for food with the seals or the eagle,

---

1. Gen 1:28.

were nevertheless a problem that sunset evening. We were exercising our rights of dominion—taking pleasure in eavesdropping on, gawking at, the private doings of animals we didn't even consider learning about beforehand. I wanted to see cute baby seals! Let's go! I want cheap energy! Let's go! I want my lifestyle! Let's go!

And yet, in the fullest sense, we, like the seals and the eagle, are not problems, not villains—we're just part of the world. We fit into nature just as much as they do. We're part of the food chain even if it's mostly microbes that get to feast on us nowadays. Our capabilities—to design watercraft that can take us out for a sunset row or around the world; to make a poison like DDT which can end the threat of malaria but endanger eagles; to do scientific research and write poetical reflections on nature; to invade the territory of other species and to coexist with them; to fight wars over oil, gold, land, or religion, and sometimes make peace; to pollute and to clean up our messes—those capabilities of ours are just as natural, just as innate, as the seals' knowing when to haul out and rest and when to get back in the water, or the eagle's knowing where to find food. Paradoxically, one of our capabilities is to envision ourselves as not part of that natural world, but above it. And, sadly, that capability could do us in, and take the rest of the world out, too.

The most ancient stories of our kind tell of the creation of the world. In so many versions, the Creator wanted a physical space to be in, to play in, to love in. We can say the universe is the Creator's self-expression. The physical world is God's body. And we, little creatures in the big starry night, we are part of that. We belong. We are part of the body of God. For Christians, God known in Jesus came and lived with us to make sure we learned the lesson well—the kingdom of God is within you! God is love, and God is with us, and God is everywhere. God is not a distant boss, with dominion over us—God didn't make us to exploit us or mistreat us—God made us for companionship—with God, with each other, with the whole world. God made us so that we could imitate God. We're God's partners. The dominion that we have is the dominion of love, the same dominion God has over us.

6

So Much History

WHAT WILL OUR THEOLOGY, our "words about God," be like when wilderness doesn't exist anymore, when the sky of stars is blotted out by streetlights and neon and searchlights, by humble porch lights that folks leave on for an idea of self-protection or from some discomfort with the blackness of the night? If, indeed, we humans can keep our whole edifice of energy going, and we are not headed for self-destruction. If rather than more and more steel and plastic and glass and screaming lights, we are headed for so much pollution and war and starvation that the "modern world" collapses and Planet Earth renews itself through another long Dark Age. But as we approach what could be this collapse, we are losing species and civilizations and races and spaces, all in the name of profit. What will be left as we head toward this transformation? What will we lose? The individual questions about mortality—my dad's, my own, Allen's, anyone's—get quickly submerged when I think about a backdrop for life that is utterly changed.

Today Dad and I both have colds. I feel pretty miserable, and I can only imagine how much worse he feels. Yesterday he was so floppy again. I was home alone with him and he could barely make it down the hall to the bathroom. His walker was canting off on tangents so that he sort of tacked first right, then left, out of the living room and through the kitchen. He couldn't stand on his own at all, so he couldn't let go of the walker and pull down his own pants.

I just said, "Dad, I'm going to do this for you, and I'll close my eyes." I did, and he sat on the toilet without protesting. When he was through, he managed to stand up on his own and get his own Depends pulled up, so I just did the pants. Glad we switched to elastic-waisted fleece pants a month ago.

Put that advice in the book of reflections for caregivers: Buy elastic-waisted pants!

I learned yesterday that the baritone Dmitri Hvorostovsky had died after two and a half years of battling brain cancer. Back when Mary and Dad and I were going to the *Met: Live in HD* events at our local cinema, he was my heart throb. (Jonas Kaufman was Mary's.) I know from watching Allen or Mary or my dad listen to music that I don't hear what they hear; I'm not musically sensitive enough. For me, the fun of the operas was the spectacle and having the shared experiences with Dad. I doubt I'll ever go to the opera again now that he can't. But that way of experiencing an opera—in a movie theater where I could nap without offending anyone (and got some of my best sleep there, during overtures), and where the subtitles made the crazy plots comprehensible, and where close-up shots meant you could see the muscles in the singers' faces and see the physical effort required to shape each note perfectly—that worked for me. To see and hear Dmitri Hvorostovsky and Renée Fleming in *Eugene Onegin* was thrilling even for me.

When I learned in 2015 that Hvorostovsky had a brain tumor, it made me really sad. Even though my experiences as a chaplain with folks who had brain cancer made me know that he would not get a cure or even much time, of course I hoped. And he seemed for a little while to be undefeated, continuing to perform and wow audiences. We were watching *Il trovatore* when he appeared as the Conte di Luna during a break in his treatment. The audience gave him an ovation when he appeared on stage, and the orchestra showered him with white roses at the opera's conclusion. Last night, Dad and I watched clips of him singing various roles on YouTube. That earlier stagger down the hall to the bathroom didn't prevent Dad from wanting also to stagger to his computer to watch the video. I stood behind Dad's chair with tears in my eyes for Hvorostovsky, for Dad, for myself.

How fitting that it would be opera that would help me cry. This art form which, for some reason, took hold of my dad as a teenager despite him growing up in an almost acultural family. His love for opera was something he shared with his maternal grandmother, something he could own that his mother wouldn't gainsay. Opera dominated Saturday afternoons throughout my childhood, my dad lounging with newspapers or a book next to the old Zenith radio that he had had since before the war. To me, then, opera appeared to involve interminable hours of shrieking and emoting that I couldn't understand. His first love, Kirsten Flagstad, was performing at the Wadsworth Atheneum in Hartford when he was a teenager at boarding school in Avon. He persuaded all the adults in his world, both his parents and the authorities at the boarding school, to let him go to hear her, sometime between 1935 and 1938. Many times he has described his fascination with her as more than just musical—as an adolescent crush.

The lush, ridiculous world of opera. I am locked out of the music, but not the drama. It will always be evocative of my dad for me, and if this present illness is the true beginning of the end for him, I will always associate it with the death of Dmitri Hvorostovsky. In one of the little intermission interviews that were added to the *Live in HD* broadcasts, Renée Fleming was asked—I can't remember by whom, but probably not another singer—"How do you get the notes timed just right?" She looked genuinely surprised, and as I remember it, said, "But that is up to the composer." And that showed me another aspect of opera: it's not all blowsy overflow, but mathematically precise. All the singers have to hit all the notes just as they were written for it to work. Like all art, it is also a craft. A discipline.

***

Dad has pulled through his cold. I am still fighting mine, the main aspect of it now being that I have lost my voice. Which, metaphorically speaking, I have been struggling not to do since I got home here. And perhaps that is even why I quit my job at the hospital, the struggle not to lose my voice. My boss there definitely wanted me to shut up. I am glad Dad has recovered, even though, of course, it is just "OK for now." Of course, of course, there will be something, my God, ad infinitum, ad nauseam, there will be something. Ninety-eight years old in a month! Yes, there will be something.

This morning brought another hard frost, although up close to the house there are still plants that show bits of green. We haven't even gotten into the teens yet, temperature-wise, let alone stayed there. When I began this record it was warm and sunny and dry, day after day, until the blue sky began to feel hostile. Then we were in a drought, and California and Oregon were on fire. Today, the silvered ground throws off blue and magenta sparks in the dawn. And with the coming of the dawn, which now is so late that I have been up for hours in the dark house, with the cat careening around me, excited by a human awake, I feel my sadness.

Yesterday afternoon my stepson Justus and his partner Julie came for a post-Thanksgiving visit to Dad. He had been too sick to really enjoy their prior visit on Thanksgiving Day itself, but was feeling better. To my surprise (and it always surprises me when this happens), during their visit he was sharp-toned when he spoke to me, only to me, and had that annoyed look on his face that I take to mean I am an idiot in his opinion. I was hurt and struggled not to show it or strike back. There were a few things that he said which were factually wrong—not significant things, just details of memory. For example, he said Dmitri Hvorostovsky grew up in the slums of a Siberian city and I disagreed, saying that his parents were professionals and he had a middle-class-sounding childhood.

Later that night, when I returned from a brief visit to Deer Isle where Justus and Julie are staying, I found Dad seated at the computer. He said sheepishly, "You were right about Hvorostovsky. But it is embarrassing to be corrected in conversation, I am afraid people will think I am a silly old man who can't keep things straight."

Wow, what an eye-opener that was for me. Here I am still fighting the battles of my youth, when both my parents dictated to me, "*This is* the way things are, you are wrong." But my dad is not in that place anymore. Now he is trying to engage meaningfully in conversation with younger people. He does a pretty good job of keeping up with them. And Justus and Julie did a good job of circling back from time to time to catch him up with what was being said.

I felt such love for Dad, and regret for my attitude, and said, "Well, you can be reassured by realizing that I think of you as a peer and don't hold back when I have a different opinion! None of this business—'Poor Old Father William, we have to make allowances . . .'" He laughed.[1]

I had a rare perspective on his distress. I am so used to taking it personally! And we have so much history.

***

The questions of mortality . . . Allen and I are watching the BBC nature documentary series *The Blue Planet* about life in the world's oceans. Penguins search far below the Antarctic ice shelves for food and leopard seal pups learn to hunt. Far to the north, polar bear cubs observe carefully as their mothers stalk prey, and, awkwardly at first, imitate their hunting

---

1. Referring to Father William was a long-standing family joke about aging, which comes from the poem by Lewis Carroll "You Are Old, Father William."

postures. Harp seal mothers and their babies haul out cautiously on the edges of ice floes for a bask in the sun. All is pristine and peaceful. There are no intruding humans with snowmobiles and rifles (at least not on camera). But wait—the scene is not so peaceful! The sweet-faced leopard seals hunt (and catch and kill and eat) the cute, comical penguins. The furry, rolypoly polar bear cubs will starve if their mothers don't nab those charming armfuls of harp seals. We humans like to edit nature so that it fits our Walt Disney vision of it, but the real story is something different.

Psalm 19 begins: "The heavens are telling the glory of God . . ."[2] Since the sun and moon and stars are, at least so far, conveniently remote, we have no idea what kinds of death or pain or interplay of competition are lived out there. And so, we happily equate the glory of God with spangled, sparkly stuff. "The firmament proclaims [God's] handiwork."

We tend to imagine that God's handiwork is either cute and snuggly or far away and pretty. That the glory of God has to do with skies and soaring heights and amazing natural wonders, right? But . . . Jesus, central teacher for Christians, was solidly earthbound, solidly commonplace in his revelation of the glory of God. His concerns were very earthbound concerns—the well-being of the poor and the outcast, and healing the sick. He talked about the love of neighbor made possible by God's love, which in turn makes justice possible. He spoke primarily to those experiencing the non-glorious side of being part of God's creation, to those who were suffering illnesses, those who were suffering ostracism and rejection at the hands of good, nice people who were the mainstream of society.

Jesus went where the earth was the muckiest, saying to prostitutes, publicans, tax collectors, and sinners, "Come have dinner with me. Be separated from God no longer—sin no more." He went also to those mired in excess, trapped by wealth and greed, and to them he said, "Give all of that up. Listen to the word of God that will free you from your possessions and your fears. Sell all you have and follow me."[3]

And he died. Just as will all the animals, all the plants, we ourselves, even the sun and the stars. Even my dad. Even me.

---

2. Ps 19:1.

3. Luke 18:22.

7

Yet Another Morning

Yet another morning when I snapped at my dad. Allen and I were leaving to get a few more little things for the Pittsburgh grandchildren who will be visiting us over Christmas. I knew that Allen would get overwhelmed and be unable to find things that he feels good about as gifts, or that work for us with our limited budget, or that I feel good about. We were given a few vague suggestions by their father, Allen's son Eben, but Allen went out shopping the other day and came home empty handed and depressed. I went yesterday and found some of what seemed like it would be good. But we needed more, and I still wanted to get a few little decorative Christmassy things too, if the price was right, so that the place Eben's family will be staying when they are here will be a bit festive. Anyway, it felt like a worthwhile use of my energy, despite my lingering cold, to go with Allen, but my dad said, "You need to be careful, don't push," and I crossly said, "I can make up my own mind." Ridiculous on my part, to take everything so damned personally all the time.

When my mom was dying, a home hospice patient with us as her caregivers, my dad spent most of every day either outside in the garden or up in his study. I, still heavily influenced by my Clinical Pastoral Education experience a few years before, tried to broker a deeper connection between them in a sort of chaplain-ish role, in a way that I would know better than to try now even as a chaplain, and certainly not for my own family members. Yeah, it would have been nice for my mom to have his companionship, but he couldn't do that. What he could do, similar in a way to what I am doing for him now, was make it possible for her to be at home during her final illness, even though he couldn't stay in the room with her for very long. Even though I was forty-six and happily married, I wanted my mommy and daddy to be in love with each other and show it. I had so many questions about their relationship, but couldn't break through our years of restraint to ask them. Plus, can a child, even in adulthood, ever really ask deep questions of their parents about the emotional texture of their parents' marriage?

I think of the suggested Al-Anon meeting welcome statement: "Living with an alcoholic is too much for most of us. Our thinking becomes distorted by trying to force solutions, and we become irritable and unreasonable without knowing it."[1] My dad is not an alcoholic, but my mom sure was. My dad is an untreated codependent, addicted to trying to manage other people's lives with the best of intentions. He is anxious, he is frightened, he is self-centered, and he is frail and vulnerable now. I try to force solutions and I am irritable and unreasonable in response to him. We are trying to out-codependent one another, it seems.

But I am the one with physical and mental energy, I am not the one trying to come to terms with my own imminent demise; although, of course, who knows if my demise is imminent or whether he is trying to come to terms with his? I am the one with years and years of therapy under my belt and I am nearly thirty-six years into my recovery from drugs and alcohol. Maybe without the therapy and those years, this situation would be far, far worse.

I need to use all the inner skills I've learned to do a better job with taking care of my dad.

***

This writing task which I set for myself, envisioned as a daily practice, has turned out to be less formal since that would become one more stressful obligation—but it feels weird when so much happens in the gaps between entries. Eben and his wife, Laura, and their two daughters, Sadie and Lucy, arrived Sunday in time for church, and our visit with them was really nice, relaxed in a way that both Allen and I experienced but couldn't figure out the cause of—was it in us, in them, in all of us? We really enjoyed the day.

1. *How Al-Anon Works*, 8.

They were in a local rental cabin, which meant that meals and playtime were with us over at Dad's house a lot of the time, so Dad saw a lot of Eben and his family. He really, really enjoyed the adult conversations and watching the children play.

I missed some of the special times, times playing outside on the icy beach or with the girls and Allen making snowpeople. I stayed behind because it didn't feel safe to leave Dad for long. Sure enough, the one time he was alone, in a two-hour stretch between when we all left for Orono to visit with James and his wife, Emily, their children, Jack and Kate, and just before—fifteen minutes before—Mary came to be with him while we were gone, he fell. He was doing something he has been advised against and nagged crossly about by me over and over—moving around without his walker. He tried to go a few steps, lost his balance, fell—once again did not get hurt. How long will we be so lucky?

He was reaching for his glasses, which were in an inconvenient spot—a place that used to work for him when he was more flexible and could reach around his body, lean over, and still maintain stability. Not anymore. An inconvenient spot that I had been guilty of utilizing for the glasses more than once myself, by his chair on a table which he keeps in a welter. And I had harped on the need to rearrange tables and lamps etc., too often for his liking, that being my fetish—let's throw everything into chaos, sort it out, and enjoy the new order. But in this case I should have prevailed—and this morning I finally have, and we have rearranged things so that all will be in reach while he is sitting in his chair. (I am well aware of how likely it is that this newly cleaned up surface will become too congested to be useful too . . .)

I haven't gotten any writing done this week. Staying up late because there are visitors means it is too hard to get up early. Not getting up early means there is too much going on to get any writing done. I've been trying to scare up a Christmas present for my aunt, Dad's eighty-two-year-old sister, who is as healthy and vital and young for her age as he has always been until recently—and still is, in many ways. I've also been making beds and tidying the living room and the bathroom for her visit. Putting away clothes, making coffee. Figuring out what we can give her for lunch. James called to see how Grandpa is doing after his fall, so we chatted. And so on.

One thing I don't want to lose track of is that the other night when I was helping my dad into bed and told him I loved him, as I do each night, he said, "That shows." Such a surprise and so lovely.

Yet Another Morning

Another thing to remark on is that finally he and the cat seem to have worked out a reasonable relationship. She now spends most of her time asleep on his lap.

***

Maybe what happens to me occasionally in the middle of the night would be termed a panic attack. I've never thought of it that way, first, because I don't consider myself to be "the kind of person who has panic attacks," and second, because there's no racing heart or sweaty palms. What there is is an overwhelming feeling of helplessness, meaninglessness, and doom. And it only seems to happen when something has awakened me and I can't get back to sleep. Maybe what wakes me up is not some noise outside, which is what I have always assumed, but the onset of the attack. When I sleep, generally I wake up stiff, with various body parts hurting, and that lasts until I move around some—so when I lie sleeplessly in bed, I become more and more aware of how much everything hurts, which only adds to the unpleasantness of not sleeping.

And in those dark hours it is hard not to brood about the overall world situation and feel despair. Racial, religious, gender-based, and ethnic prejudice and violence now exacerbated by climate change, our planetary "new normal"—climate change and the disasters it wreaks on the nonhuman world in addition to the suffering it causes humans—humans who mostly live in places other than rural Maine. Mostly humans in poorer economic classes than mine, which would be low-middle class by income, despite my incredibly privileged class position in terms of education, health, and potential to inherit property and money. It is hard to look at my four grandchildren—who are growing up thus far in ideal conditions with educated, sensible parents who are giving them all kinds of advantages, including not giving them too many advantages—and not worry about how our planet is undergoing climate change and a global shift to right-wing paranoia and selfishness.

During the day, I can usually fend off thoughts of despair about the world by historical contextualizing. But that isn't working so well right now, even during the day, and it definitely doesn't work at night as it is easy to think, "Yup, we've always been screwed up and it is a mystery why we even exist. What a waste of space the human race is. Waste of resources, the planet would be better off without us, with our AI and our nuclear bombs and our pollution and our mass killings of one another, and of birds, animals, and marine life."

A Matter of Death and Life

***

For many of my generation, and for our generation's offspring, the *Lord of the Rings Trilogy* by J. R. R. Tolkien has been taken with great seriousness as far more revelatory of the way good and evil work in the world than any of the apocalyptic writing in the Bible. The basic plot: Frodo and his friends must travel from their pleasant and safe-seeming homes to the kingdom of an evil wizard and destroy a magical ring that has come into Frodo's possession. If it is not destroyed, then the evil wizard will overtake the whole world. Their journey, their task, is nearly impossible; but if they succeed, evil will be vanquished forever. They have to do the hardest thing imaginable, suffer terribly, risk life and limb and sanity—but they only have to do one thing: see that the ring is destroyed.

If only. If only it were that easy! "Your task is to do the one most impossible thing. Be the hero, in a big way, one time only, and save the world." Instead, life is made up of many, many tasks, daily tasks of varying possibility and impossibility, and evil is far too complex to vanquish completely. "Kill Hitler, get rid of Saddam Hussein, oust Pinochet or De Klerk or Mugabe, catch Osama bin Laden, elect a Democrat, elect a Republican . . ." Some of those evil wizards are gone now, but the world has not become a perfect place.

As much as we want to locate evil somewhere specific, in a particular person, in a particular ideology, in a particular circumstance, we find that evil is a lot more subtle than that. Evil exists intertwined with good, and evil and goodness exist within us all. It's not always easy to identify evil; and what is clearly evil in the eyes of one person is not so bad, or is even good, in the eyes of another.

So much of our iconography, our mythology, our theology, the fairy tales we read to children, the movie plots we love so well, novels, poetry, drama, music, is motivated by this theme: do the one impossible thing and the world will be redeemed. Even the story of Jesus can be read that way—die on a cross, make everything right for humankind forever. But, if we can believe the Gospel writers, what Jesus said was not, "*Die on a* cross," but rather, "*Take up* [your] cross, and follow me."[2]

Jesus told his hearers, tells us, to follow him to wherever there is human need and serve one another. The big gesture, the one-time performance of the impossible task is not the point of the story of Jesus, even though there

---

2. Matt 16:24b.

is much church teaching that would make it seem so. There is much church teaching that would have us believe that since Jesus already did the one impossible thing, dying for our sins to appease God on our behalf, we don't have to worry about the details of trying to live as Jesus asked his followers to do. In that scenario, Jesus is the hero in a battle between good and evil, and all we have to do is keep our heads down and stay out of the way, being grateful to him, adoring him, but basically living in whatever way pleases us.

For the earliest Christian thinkers that kind of relationship with Jesus would have been unimaginable. They carefully preserved for us Jesus's teachings, his message of service and humility. Take up your cross, shoulder the burden, or the responsibility, of being human—the ambiguity, the difficulty, the unfairness, and the plain hard work of being human. Shoulder the burden of living with doubt and uncertainty. Live at times with these questions: Where is God? How can God let this evil happen?

We look around us at the world in which innocent people suffer terribly and we wonder, Where is God? Where is God for the homeless man, the battered woman, the abused child? Where is God in the war zone or the refugee camp? When human suffering is so extreme, why doesn't God intervene? In the long-ago words of the prophet Isaiah, "Oh, that you would tear open the heavens and come down . . ."[3]

How we wish it could be so. To have God show up and set things to rights. To make the world a better place, a kinder place, a place with more peace, more love, justice. To have God show up and give us a mission, a plan, a blueprint, so that *we* could set things to rights, destroy the Ring, kill the evil wizard, annihilate evil once and for all. But—wait a minute—don't we already have a mission, a plan, and a blueprint? Doesn't it go something like: Love God with all your heart and soul and mind and strength, and your neighbor as yourself?[4]

***

And now it is three days before Christmas. I have been feeling much happier, actually, than I was this time last year. I was still at the big city hospital and I'd just had my pivotal, unexpected, and really distressing encounter with my boss, in which she came up to the pediatric ICU to order me to leave the bedside of a child who had just been declared brain dead and was

3. Isa 64:1a.
4. Matt 22:37–39.

going to be allowed to die. My boss ordered me to leave the family and go to Operational Excellence training. I quietly declined her order, saying, "No, I am sorry, I can't do that," and stayed with the family. After all was said and done, my boss ended up apologizing to me.

Last year at this time, I resolved that if she spoke that way to me again, I would be through. And when she did it again a month later, I quit. That whole year, 2017, was a year full of changes and a year I am glad to leave behind. Quitting that job had a dreamlike quality to it because it didn't feel as if I had thought it out or planned it; nonetheless it felt right and worked out well, in the sense that I am back here in time to help Dad as he moves deeper into his end of life, and to learn more while doing that about who I am and what is important to me.

***

We are waiting for a big snowstorm, to be followed by a big rainstorm, and then more snow and freezing rain and so on.

This morning, Dad told me that he dreamed of Allen's mother Julia (who died a few years ago) last night. She was offering a workshop he really wanted to take. But he didn't have good clear directions to the workshop location, and everywhere he went he found himself in a blasted urban landscape in terrible disrepair. He asked various people for new directions and everything he was told took him down one-way streets and streets without good paving. He didn't seem to see anything particularly symbolic or significant about the dream, but I sure did. It sounds so much like a man trying to get to "the good death" that has already been completed by Julia.

Or, at least Dad thinks of it as a good death. I don't know if it was. I don't think Dad could think that way about my mother's death or his own mother's death, both because he experienced the loss of them as people, and because he saw the process of their declines. Julia's death can be an abstraction for him.

The winter solstice came and went, and we added two seconds of daylight. The chart of day length, which has read "minus," "minus," "minus" for months, now reads "plus," "plus," "plus." In ten more days, we will have added four minutes. I actually like the time of the deepening dark and don't mind short hours of daylight, but basically, my awareness of the passage of the sun and the earth through the heavens thrills me. These days I have time to be aware and to settle into open receptivity. And maybe this year is also significant because it has a feeling of maybe being the *last*: the last

Yet Another Morning

Thanksgiving, the last winter solstice, the last Christmas, the last birthday for my dad. For my dad and me with him. Hopefully not for me as an individual, except in the sense of the last time I will experience these things as the daughter of a living person.

When I see the grandchildren, the little girl I was in the 1950s seems very far away. The world seems like it was a simpler place then. My parents never taught me to believe in Santa Claus, and I couldn't really tell you what the magic of Christmas was for me, but I remember my intense feelings of joy and wonder, and the rituals that gave it meaning—my own private rituals, like lying under the Christmas tree and staring upward through its branches, and the breathless excitement of seeing the department store windows on Fifth Avenue in New York City with their animated winter scenes. I don't remember if Baby Jesus was important to me, I think I actually resented him for most of my childhood. I think I was jealous of him. He seemed like he had it pretty good, being God and all. It wasn't until seminary that I made peace with him. I made peace with him by coming to understand him as a young revolutionary, a man obedient to God, a man revealing God, and willing to be killed for his beliefs and his efforts on behalf of his people—not wanting to be killed, but aware of it as a likely consequence, and nonetheless steadfast.

8

Christmas and a New Year

ALONG WITH HIS WEDDING anniversary on December 3 (sixty-eight years since my parents' marriage in 1949), his ninety-eighth birthday on December 29, and Christmas, my dad is thinking about December 7, 1941, and the attack on Pearl Harbor. He was in his senior year at Washington and Lee, a politically aware and thoughtful young man watching Hitler's advance in Europe with horror. "After Pearl Harbor," he says, "we all knew where we were going when we graduated."

Dad is reading a new biography of Franklin Delano Roosevelt and recalling those times. I am reading *Prairie Fires*, a new biography of Laura Ingalls Wilder, with much in it about her daughter, Rose Wilder Lane, and much about the same time period as Dad's FDR book. Rose Wilder Lane was an arch-opponent of FDR and all he stood for, and an early Libertarian, as well as apparently mentally unstable. Her mother, Laura Ingalls Wilder, not surprisingly was an old-fashioned populist whose values sound a lot like those of my mother's father, my grandfather Guy Hettema, who was conservative and fearful of "alien others," but more untutored than committed to prejudice, and actually very friendly and gregarious to real, actual people instead of imagined ones.

How did my mom, coming from that kind of family, and my dad, coming from his fearful and insular family, develop into people who lived in Greenwich Village and were proud to call themselves intellectuals?

Christmas and a New Year

Yesterday I was aware of being happy and contented while I was doing little holiday tasks like making my mom's recipe for butter cookies rolled in powdered sugar, wrapping the few presents we have for the grandchildren, and writing checks for the charitable donations we make in honor of our adult children. We had bought the three-foot-high, artificial Christmas tree I coveted for Eben's family's visit (on sale at Rite-Aid for twelve dollars) and now it is here at Dad's. Allen put lights on two trees outside the house.

In this final week of 2017, I have a lot for which I feel grateful and I have a lot of sorrow for the state of the world. I guess I am in the right profession, as the combination of reflection and action that is required to be any good at ministry suits me well. To mine the Scriptures for glimpses of God. To find words for the sunlight touching the tops of the trees. To find words for the cruelty and the depravity of the way those of us with power treat those of us without it. To accompany people wherever I intersect with them on their journey from unknown life in the womb to unknown afterward. On my own journey from unknown to unknown.

Maybe this is my dad's last Christmas. Or his last Christmas with any quality of life. Maybe I have gotten to the place I hoped for that seemed so unattainable last summer, the place where I can feel affection and tenderness toward him far oftener than irritation and resentment. I realized this morning that if that is indeed true, that I feel love more than anger, it is not because he has changed, but because I have. Of course, this is exactly what the wise people of all the ages, including Bill Wilson, one of the founders of Alcoholics Anonymous, have said. You can only change yourself and the way you look at things; you can't change other people. Is there a way to extrapolate personal change to the changing of the world? Because the threats of climate change and nuclear war, not to mention the ancient pervasive realities of racism and violence to girls and women, to gay people, to animals, to babies, to the differently abled, and to the elderly are not just things that I can adopt a different outlook on, there is an objective reality that has to be addressed. Certainly, having more peace in my heart will help me, but is my inner peace helpful to others? I think so.

Looking in last year's journal to see where my thinking was at Christmas 2016, still at the big city hospital, I read this:

> When I have a day of patient tragedies, I go home exhausted but thinking about meaning, compassion, grace, and truth. When I have a day of departmental, bureaucratic, office politics/machinations, I go home exhausted and thinking about the futility of life!

Dad clearly enjoyed having great-grandkids here for New Year's Eve, but the fun also made him tired, and he seemed sad too. Maybe he just felt fatigued, or maybe he felt a sense of "This could be the last time." He is having a flare-up of a mysterious intermittent pain in his chest wall, for which he has been to the emergency room in the past and read about over and over online, as well as talked about with his primary care doc and Veterans Administration doc. He doesn't remember that he has had those conversations so he got very cross with me as I was getting (unnecessarily) cross with him about it yesterday. He wouldn't take any Tylenol, wouldn't put on a lidocaine patch. In fact, he wanted to throw all the patches away as the date on the package said they expired in 2016.

James and I both told him that they would be fine and still work. He wouldn't believe me but he believed James, which, of course, infuriated me . . .

Why was I so very cross about the whole thing? Maybe because the caregiving has been in a quiescent phase for a while. We have our routines and he doesn't seem to be deteriorating the way he was last summer. He has recovered a degree of his ability to care for himself and not lost anything new, and we aren't having out-and-out conflicts over money or my hiring of an occasional caregiver. Maybe it's just because I don't want him to develop bigger needs again and I know he most likely will. Whatever the reason, it amounted to me being brusque and unsympathetic to his obvious pain. He winces when he moves.

I know that whatever else is going on, his obsession with his symptoms and his inability to just accept the mysteries of his human body are lifelong, not new; and I share those preoccupations myself, about my own body; but I am trying so hard to unlearn them, or at least trying hard not to give them more energy.

***

Awaiting another blizzard. I wonder why I am spending more and more early morning time goofing around on the internet. It is harder to get to this writing than it was last fall. And it is harder to write about Dad. Partly, I guess, because there is such a sameness to this situation—his deterioration as slow and mysterious as ever, my feelings of love or impatience or irritation or empathy the same as ever, too. His pain of the other day seems to have subsided, but the effort for him of actually moving his body through space is so evident. Very little seems to give him pleasure. I wish for his sake he could have died during the former administration! What is coming out of the White House now, what has been done and may be done, is very depressing to Dad (to me, too).

One of the things that Dad is lacking is a sense of purpose, which I think must be hard to muster for anyone who doesn't have much physical energy. And he is not just lacking in physical energy, but also in time—life's window until mortality's conclusion is growing smaller and smaller for him. Smaller and smaller based on logic, though not based on a diagnosis, or any advance of specific symptoms.

***

My work as a pediatric chaplain was not a happy job, but it was a very rewarding one. And I did find many ways to make it happy in the relationships I had with medical staff and families, as well as with my young patients when they were able to be interested in engaging with me. I have made my life happy a lot of the time through fostering relationships and drawing meaning from the experiences I have. Being a chaplain gave me joy, even though it was not joyful work. And I could leave it behind to a certain extent whenever I left the hospital at day's end, even though some of the memories of the patients and the families and the staff will always be with me. I wish that I could say of this caregiving work I do with Dad now that it is rewarding, that it gives me a certain kind of joy. But I can never leave it behind at the end of a day, I have nowhere to go that doesn't include my awareness that my dad is dying.

Dad woke up in a better place than he was in last night. There isn't any reason I can discern for that, but I am glad. When I hear his voice cutting in to my early morning reveries with a querulous "Hello?" I always feel such flaming annoyance. In that early morning time, I am managing my own anxiety, not his. Will the day come when I don't hear his voice and just assume, with gratitude, that he is sleeping in, and then eventually on that future morning, go in to check on him and see that he has died? Will I feel horribly ashamed? I am sure I will feel loss and probably also relief. For now, though, his actual death is so theoretical most of the time, and the habit of feeling invaded by him is so very familiar, that I feel aggravation when he wakes up. But today he woke up in a decent mood even though he commented at breakfast that it had been very hard to get out of bed, physically and mentally. I was able to feel compassion for him and not feel that I had to somehow cheer him up, cheer him on. To just be present with him.

It is eight below, cloudy, and might snow in a bit. It did snow overnight. Deep winter. I am glad to be at home in Brooklin with Allen and Dad instead of house-sitting in Yarmouth or any of the other places I bounced around in in southern Maine for six years. Although I am still sorry to have left the hospital, still missing the work I was doing, I am so glad to be away from the stress. I remember feeling that way during my chaplain residency in Connecticut too. The work there was even more demanding—a bigger place by far, twice the size—and I was a beginner. In both jobs, it is hard to separate what was hard about the patient-care work from what was hard about the institutional politics, and to separate both those things from the lifestyle I led because of my small income.

What is on my mind this New Year's time is meaning-making, and what it implies. There are events and activities that provide significance that is so obvious that their meaning is unquestioned by anyone. People in all walks of life do these large and important things. But there are far more times in human lives without that order of magnitude. It is a challenge to see what is significant, even extraordinary, in little moments—to see the beauty of an icy leaf, to hear the reassuring thunder of the oil burner coming on, to share a smile over the breakfast table. It is a challenge to be obedient to the doing of all the mundane tasks that fill our days, rather than being fretful, yearning for more, for bigger tasks. It is a challenge to do the small things over and over, attempting an attitude of patience and compassion rather than being restless and . . . yearning for more, once again.

What is "meaning" when there doesn't seem to be any meaning? At the very least, perhaps, there is meaning in living the kind of life that most people throughout history ever live—taking care of the children and the elders and the animals, cleaning up, making meals, staying warm and dry. Most people *yearn* to live that kind of life, I should say, as they struggle with war and loss and prejudice and genocide and poverty. And maybe that is a more appropriate kind of yearning, for basic needs to be met, than my kind of yearning—to be important, significant, have Big Experiences. Kind of like wanting a perpetual acid trip.

When I went to Connecticut to do my year of residency as a chaplain in 1991, I went with the same bravado I had when I was interviewing for ministerial jobs at churches in different parts of Maine. *At the end of this time, I will settle here for a job. I will do it, even though it means leaving the support system of family and friends, of sky and sea, that has been home for so long*, I was thinking. And at the end of the residency, I learned of a good chaplain job at a nearby rehab hospital, a job I could probably have been hired for, but I bailed and came back to Maine where I then had seven years of low-paid non-chaplain work before I really began my career in ministry.

Which brings me back to—meaning. To the suffering of the world and my desire to be of some use to it. To my fear that as a matter of convenience or timidity I am not allowing myself to hear God's "call." To my impatience with my ego-driven need to paint on a big canvas. To not allowing myself to acknowledge that God sometimes can call us into uncertainty and worldly insignificance.

The challenge is to be open. And perhaps to risk "not-risking."

Why is it that I avoid writing much about patients I've served as a chaplain? On some level, it seems that would be exploitative and voyeuristic. The folks who let me into their lives for what comfort I could give were not expecting to be written up, even in an anonymized form. And my goal when I was with them was to be *with* them. Not to gather up something for myself, although, of course, I couldn't have kept doing the work if it hadn't met a need of mine, too.

I have notes from the beginning of my job as pediatric chaplain at the big hospital, in a new position which I largely created, notes I kept as I wanted to see if I was actually *doing* anything valuable, since my way of being a chaplain was so much about just showing up and accompanying people in terrible pain, in spiritual despair, in loss and grief—not pursuing a religious agenda, for sure, and not even really having a care agenda. I was simply doing my best to respond as needed, going deeper when possible. That meant being around on the floors a lot so staff would think of me as a resource and I could familiarize myself with where the tough cases were likely to be on a given day.

My memories are specific. Standing in the visitor parking garage with a young parent recently arrived from a foreign country while his little girl was dying from a horrible disease. The parent was chain-smoking, and all of us staff members were supposed to intervene politely and prevent people from smoking on hospital grounds. Not a chance. I would have defended that parent's right to smoke to any policymaker at the hospital. I listened while he talked and tried not to inhale any of the smoke myself.

Standing with an attending physician, a registered nurse, a child life worker, a certified nursing assistant, a resident physician, and two parents while their baby, born with countless problems, died in his mother's arms after a few months of life that had been spent mostly in the intensive care unit. We stood together for hours, it seemed, all of us absolutely still, keeping the baby comfortable, but watching him die, his lungs not able to work even with massive amounts of oxygen. Just watching the baby, watching the parents watching their baby. Watching the doctors watching the baby.

Sitting with a Muslim father while his Christian wife grieved violently for their nearly full-term baby who had died in utero. She spoke no English, and she didn't need to. She was so far away in her grief that she wouldn't have heard anything said to her anyway. He told me of their difficult journey to leave their home, of their difficult journey to become pregnant, and of their family on the other side of the world.

Arguing fiercely with willing but uninformed staff about not putting a dead toddler into a body bag in front of his parents. Telling them that, yes, the little one could go to the morgue under his blankie and be bagged for the funeral home down there. Arguing fiercely over and over again with the security staff, with the Health Information Management staff, interpreting Maine law for them, waving policies and statutes around in partnership with indignant nurses and frustrated doctors, all of us trying to break the bureaucratic logjam so that Muslim families could take their dead baby away with them for proper burial.

Talking to the Muslim elders and finally becoming the hospital "expert" on Muslim burial customs, despite how much I didn't know.

Going in and out of the morgue with the pathologists, who weren't sure what to make of the fact that my care of families included, had to include, ongoing proximity to their loved ones' dead bodies. I had to assure families that their baby's body was still there, so that when the mother came out of her coma after a car accident she could see her dead child; I had to pray over a body while an out-of-state extended family assembled; I monitored the gradual decomposition of an unembalmed body so that a family could be helped to let a loved one go without a key person having the chance for a viewing if it was all taking too long.

***

Yesterday and today I just feel so sad, so out of sorts. Allen is offshore at his part-time ministry job and I miss him. Last night, I smelled smoke in the middle of the night and was pretty sure it was the neighbors' woodstove; but I got up and walked around sniffing and looking as quietly as I could, so as not to wake up Dad, for a possible source of the smell. Then couldn't get back to sleep for a long time. I had the hopeless, sad, meaningless feeling I often do, and also wondered yet again why my body hurts so much these days. I wonder if it is "just" a reaction to the ongoing stress of caregiving.

I think too much about death: my own, my dad's, the death of the planet. I have the feeling that things are spinning faster and faster into absurdity and danger.

I spoke with my friend Mary about caregiving, asking her if when she was taking care of her mother, who had dementia and died at age 102, she worried more than usual about her own health and her own death. Her response: "Do you even have to ask? Of course I did!" As is so often true for us, we ended up laughing together about our fears and projections and the state of the world and our hopes for it.

**

Allen and I had a night away, one that was difficult to arrange and bring off. And when we got home from that yesterday, Dad was almost pitifully glad to see me, even though he had been first with James and then with Mary, two people with whom he has a high degree of comfort. He sort of clung to me when I kissed him hello. He expressed interest in our trip and seemed fine, but after he took a nap, he woke up chilled and very, very grumpy. I began to wonder if maybe he was sick, since he was so cold and so grumpy, but didn't quite move on it. Instead, I worked on getting him warmed up, made him dinner, fixed up his bed.

After eating, he wasn't interested in the news, but sat there with his eyes closed until, at seven o'clock, he said was going to go to bed. That's when I decided to take his temperature. Lo and behold, it was 101 degrees. So I gave him Tylenol and he started to get up and walk to the bathroom, but got only a few steps and stalled, couldn't move his feet. His legs began bending sideways and he was swaying. Because he was holding on to the walker he didn't fall, thankfully. I called out for Allen, who came downstairs and got in position to steady Dad. I was able to put a chair under Dad, and he sat by his walker in the living room to do his teeth with a bowl, water, and towel—did his entire mouthwash routine. Eventually we got him under the covers in bed and he fell asleep quickly.

The last thing he said to me was that we should be sure to watch *Washington Week* as they would have good commentary on the President's latest horrible racist remarks about African countries and about how Haiti was a horrible, unlivable place. I reassured him that we would, and we did have it on, but I found it more important to get James's take on things about Dad than to listen to the talking heads. James was serious about it—warned me not to think of this as something that would pass quickly; given Grandpa's age, he said, this could be the true "beginning of the end." He said if it is bacterial, he will need antibiotics; if it is viral, he will get so weak that all kinds of things could happen. He said, "If you decide not to go to the hospital tomorrow, know that is like making the big decision for 'comfort care only.'"

I asked him if he thought I should put that decision—hospital or not—to Grandpa in just those terms, and he said yes. So, I heard all that, but still believed last night, and do even more so this morning after a quiet night, that Dad will shake this off. What I think is happening is that I was away from him for twenty-four hours and he couldn't take the anxiety of that. It wore down his resistance to germs.

I don't think he deliberately punishes me by getting sick, but it amounts to the same thing, as I now feel like I can't go away overnight again—ever. Or else he will get sick and if he does, at some point, he won't be able to shake it off. Maybe at some point I will go away anyway, and he will get sick and die. Because I can't prevent him from being mortal, and I can't not live my life just because he is dependent on me or because he is afraid.

Allen slept downstairs in case Dad needed him, and that was a huge help to me because I can't sleep in the recliner chair and because I can't help Dad with the commode anyway. Allen being cheerfully willing to do things like that is vastly more helpful than his slow response to a crisis is harmful. I am glad I know that. I am glad both Allen and I can acknowledge that my crisis assessment and response is quicker than his and not make a power struggle out of it. Once upon a time I think we would have, with me being really annoyed and expecting him to smarten up and him being extremely defensive and disagreeing with me about what was actually happening, what was needed, and so on. Now we both just know that I will suss out what is going on in any situation and call it out more quickly than he does, and then we will work together to address things. We both know, too, that Allen has strengths that I don't have.

This morning I have spoken with Dad, who says he is not in any pain but feels wiped out. Since he usually feels wiped out and never remembers that he usually feels that way, his saying that, so far, doesn't seem significant to me. He was cool to the touch, so I doubt he has a fever anymore. When he truly wakes up and gets up, we may be in the scenario James was describing, where the fact of having the fever and perhaps his immune system being in a fight-germs mode will mean that he is too weak to get himself around.

That will be a bridge to cross. I don't think I would take him to the emergency room with no symptoms but weakness and a fever last night, because even at ninety-eight, I don't think that would be considered "admittable," and it would take all day to be told that. Especially not during a busy flu season—to which he might be more exposed there than at home.

This morning I am aware of my own fatigue. Aware of Allen and myself not being as young as we once were, and more susceptible to flu and other conditions ourselves. I am aware of resentment, of the feeling of being on a merry-go-round. Of feeling trapped. But last night, when Dad was so out of it and couldn't really move around and had a fever—last night I thought, *Oh shit, this is it! Have I said and done everything significant and important?* I felt that sense of slow-motion unreality that goes with watching a disaster unfold. When I went upstairs to go to bed, I felt oppressed by all the things in this house that I will have to deal with when Dad dies, things I can put off dealing with now because they are still his things, not mine yet. And I felt sad, so deeply sad, to think that he was dying and would be gone from me forever.

All of this is true at the same time, the resentment and feeling of being burdened—the weariness of all the tasks—the sorrow and the loss.

When I think he might be actually dying, I am aware of the abyss and the unfathomable nature of death, and the vastness of impending loss and the transformation it will wreak in me. When I think he is just proceeding along, slowly, through his aging process, I so often feel resentment. The duality of the experience gives me a kind of permission from the universe to be my same old self, immature and selfish one moment, compassionate and self-sacrificing the next. I'm having the feeling of being child to his adult, as well as the feeling of being child to his child. Adult to his child. And sometimes, adult to his adult. Basically, I feel either resentful and self-pitying, or guilty and afraid.

There are things in the world to be afraid of and to prepare for. But due to my childhood conditioning—watching and listening to my dad's fears—and perhaps my genes, and to my own experiences of being in way over my head and on my own too often as a little child, my interior, distant, early-warning system is on Red Alert much of the time. Like my dad's hyped-up internal warning system, except about more actually dangerous things like fires and nuclear attacks, things with more consequence than his endless litany: "The rugs are being ruined by my walker" (not true), "James should not moonlight at the little local hospital as the hospital that employs him full time plans for him to have time off" (also not true), "Allen should not shovel snow" (possibly true), and so forth. I feel like my dad has spent so much of his life aroused by fear that his ability to detect actual threat is mostly absent, and I think, I hope, that that is not true for me.

I have thought a lot about making preparations for disasters of various types. It is true that I am on hair-trigger alert for these sorts of things, which has been both helpful and harmful, though neither in an all-consuming way. I haven't averted any major disasters and I haven't caused any. But I have made my life more agitated and more complicated at times. I can almost see the spiral I could go down, where there is never enough preparation for something; for example, for a nuclear war, you need to have shelter, food, water, medical supplies, clothes, a way to poop, a way to communicate, something to sit on, somewhere to sleep—and your very survival could go all the way to needing a way to kill your neighbors if they come asking that you share food, water, medicine, and more. And to what end would I be saving myself and my family? Life in a destroyed world with none of what is precious and valuable now, most likely. I could go the survivalist route and make my whole life be about protecting myself from something unnamed and unnameable, because I don't think I could pick a villain like the North Koreans or the immigrants or the FBI/CIA/POTUS/whatever alphabet soup is supposed to be my "righteous" target. I'm not interested in protecting myself for the sake of something to do—or wanting to live in a state of crisis and be absorbed by that as a way of avoiding having an actual complex-though-not-always-satisfying life that will end in death at some point no matter what I do.

And that is the deal, probably, actually—the old mortality thing. The old "I don't want to die; I don't want to be as alone as dying and death are."

The iconography of nuclear war permeated so much of the culture of my childhood and adolescence that it is an issue which has colored my thinking my whole life. I remember that when I was coming to terms with the fact that my mother was dying twenty years ago, the first image I had was of the annihilation of nuclear war—of a universe destroyed. Which in a metaphorical sense it was, as it will be when my dad dies, and when I die. Each one of us contains a universe. And such universes are continually being destroyed, as utterly and totally as in a nuclear holocaust. But unlike nuclear war, death is a good thing, generally speaking, a good thing for the planet and a good thing for the individual. The goodness of limitations.

***

Monday I went to babysit in Orono, to spend time playing with Jack and Kate. We made our favorite fort by draping blankets over the edges of their bunk beds, filled it with stuffed animals, a large cardboard box, many pillows, and, for a while, one of their cats. The kids were both sleepy from staying up late the night before, and our time in the dark, warm fort was very peaceful. As happens so often, they wanted to hear stories about James, me, and themselves. As I ran out of ideas and stories I asked them to tell me their earliest memories and told them mine.

Jack said, "I remember you pushing me in my stroller." That may be because the last time we told stories I told him I used to get him to sleep as a baby and toddler by putting him in his stroller and making figure eights out on the front porch in the streetlight-lit darkness. I would love to think that he actually has some kind of memory of those times, which were so peaceful, times when I sang and walked until he fell asleep. It may be that me mentioning these experiences made him reflect on the past and remember too, or it may be that he could visualize it when I described it, so now it is that kind of a memory—a created one.

While I was having that gentle, restorative time in Orono, Allen was home with Dad, who said, "I am having a relapse," and took some Tylenol. Allen didn't explore with him what he meant by that or take his temperature, so it is hard to know what was going on—but it is also hard for me not to believe that, once again, Dad resented my absence from him. Or maybe me being gone just makes him afraid. I would not have known any of this unless Allen had told me, because Dad said nothing about it when I saw him later. He seemed like his usual self when I got home in time for supper and the evening's television-watching. And then the next day, Dad was perky and bright when he woke and washed the lower half of his body, including his feet, without any assistance from anyone.

Normally I ask Allen to help Dad wash in case he falls. But Allen wasn't home and I decided not to argue with Dad about the process of bathing. I am tired of struggling with him about such matters and decided that, if he fell, we would just have to call 911 and get help, and so be it.

On we go, one day at a time.

9

The Bad Mood Persists

2018

Yesterday was a discombobulated day, all day long. Dad slept really late, and just as with a baby, you celebrate this and enjoy it and dread it ending. But of course, with Dad, I worried about why he was sleeping so late and, sure enough, when he did wake up he said he'd had a terrible night but couldn't be specific about why. Upshot was a trip to the doctor to learn that nothing was wrong. As often happens, he calmed down and felt fine once he was told that. Allen and I were both hoping something *would* be wrong, something minor that would put him in the hospital for a few days, so we could get a small break from caregiving.

A big chunk of the day was taken up with all of this. It was a gorgeous, mild, post-snowstorm day, but we didn't get to enjoy it much. Another part of the day was taken up with Dad having lost a bill, which we finally discovered he had paid several weeks ago—in the process of looking through his muddle of papers, I discovered that he had neglected to pay a different bill, and had to make a series of phone calls to straighten that out.

Last night I thought about how, in this writing, I am taking possession of Dad's story as it intersects with mine, for my own ends, in the same way that my mother's journals became my property to do with as I wish after she died. Maybe writers and artists always do this; maybe that is an intrinsic selfishness of art. It hadn't occurred to me before last night, though—to be

The Bad Mood Persists

revealing so many negative things about him, about my family life as a little girl. To what end? Maybe it will help somebody to read about them? That is the hope, anyway.

***

What is wrong with me? The bad mood persists. I know that I have so much to be grateful for, and dimly, as if across a chasm, I see all of it but can't get there, to well-being and gratitude. Is this just caregiver burnout? Popular wisdom says that it is not the physical tasks but the emotional drain that makes caregiving so stressful.

Allen comments on my dad's invasiveness, on his apparent need to latch on to others' lives, so that Dad's questions about what you have done during the day feel like being pried open, and rather than feeling that he is interested, oh how nice, you feel self-protective and unwilling to share. I have seen this prying in operation when he's speaking with Allen. When I see it, I feel bad for my dad, knowing that he thinks he is just being interested, polite, or whatever. Since he is picking up on Allen's resistance and can't understand it, he obviously feels hurt. And then I feel protective of Dad and annoyed with Allen. But then the next round is Dad doing the same thing to me and I am in the resister role.

It occurs to me that these extremely raw and angry feelings are percolating in me at the end of a week that began with my dad running a fever of 101, having a cough, and seeming ill until we finally had the doctor visit in which it turned out that nothing was wrong with him. On the rare occasions when my dad has voiced insight into himself and his motivations, he has more than once commented on how he gets himself all worked up. The miraculous way that even his cough stopped as soon as he saw the doctor seems to be evidence of this. But what I can't get at is what goes on in me, other than the contradictory feelings of hope that "this will be it" and fear that "this will be it." At the end of a week of trying to figure out what is going on for him and how to respond to it, I am depleted.

Since Dad's condition has turned out, once again, to be nothing, there isn't any outpouring of love and support from others. In fact, they didn't even notice. Allen and I remain in the lonely position of providing ongoing care, being in the here and now with it, and for me, also anticipating the grief, the loss that will come when he dies. Throughout all of this is the rumble of the past with its power, and the repeating refrains of the caregiving in the present.

In my present feeling state everything feels futile. I have started transcribing my mother's journals again, since I only got as far as the early 1950s before I stopped working on them ten years ago. Now there are forty more years left to go of her record of her life, although she wrote much less after she married and I was born. She stopped writing altogether when she began to feel so poorly in February 1995; she got her cancer diagnosis in August 1996 and died February 2, 1997, on her eighty-sixth birthday. Her diagnosis seemed to happen in slow motion. Her main symptom, shortness of breath, was written off by every medical professional who saw her as "not lung cancer" since no discrete mass ever showed up on an X-ray. "Oh, whoops, it was lung cancer after all," they finally told us, bronchioloalveolar cancer which doesn't show up as a mass. Instead, it presents in many, many small tumors seeded throughout the lungs.

I am glad, I think, that we didn't find out about her cancer any sooner as there wasn't any treatment they could offer to her at that time. Since there are no entries in her journals after 1995, I have no record of how she felt as her disease progressed from the time of the diagnosis. She went right into hospice care at home and lived for only five more months.

But as I type her entries—more or less one a year once we get into the part of her life where she was a wife and a mother—and as I compare them with my memories (I'm up to 1958, when I was seven), I feel depressed. I remember things so differently from the charming way she portrays our life in the suburbs where we didn't fit in, didn't have enough money or the right politics—literally, the Right. My politically liberal, intellectual parents might have been much happier and much more social had they stayed in New York City where they lived after the War, but when I came along they wanted to provide me with green suburban grass. Thus, we came to the land of country clubs and coffee-drinking, bridge-playing, stay-at-home wives married to advertising executives and businessmen, who were making a lot more money than my parents did.

And we, the privileged children of those people, so many of us, got so thoroughly into drugs in the late 1960s. We were lucky that those drugs were not the same ones thrill-seeking, unhappy, self-medicating teenagers find today. I read my mother's accounts of "happy family time" with her sisters, brothers-in-law, and their children—my cousins—and I think about the way it felt when the grown-ups and the older cousins were drinking, or about how I finally got some respectful interest from those older cousins when they realized I could tell them about drugs. I think about the tension between my parents over my mom's drinking; I think about the time, years and years later after her death, when I asked my dad what their relationship had been like at the beginning of their life together, "before she was in the grip of her drinking," I said. His candid reply: "She was always in the grip of her drinking."

Does the feeling of futility just go along with the fatigue of caregiving, such that everything, life itself, feels rather pointless and ends in the grave after whatever amount of difficulty and disappointment? Or is this mood more related to growing up in a dysfunctional family?

Or both.

Reading caregiver resource sheets on the internet helps. I "know" I am not alone in my feelings, "know" they go with the territory—but I need to be reminded. It is hard to keep perspective on the normality of my feelings of anger, resentment, and being overwhelmed. There has been a well of resentment and anger in me for years. Being aware of it has only been a positive thing, ultimately, since I can work on it, even though feeling it is so very hard. But not being in touch with it only meant that its effects happened underground in me, it didn't mean that the feelings weren't there.

***

The hard emotional work of recognizing what was going on in me and naming it as emotional exhaustion resulting from a week of wondering what was going on with Dad health-wise, my complicated feelings of wanting him to die and being afraid of it, feeling resentment, grief, regret, sorrow etc., paid off. I have not flamed out in angry, demanding emails or phone calls to anyone, trying to make someone else take on my emotional challenges. Once I was grounded again it was easy to check in with James, who has a very demanding work schedule right now with a string of midnight-to-eight-a.m. shifts in a row, and catch him up on Grandpa's condition and on mine. It also helped to read yet another article online about caregiver stress that listed all the things that I was feeling: the resentment, the inadequacy, the futility, the isolation.

It helped that after Allen left for his job offshore, Dad and I started getting along better, as so often happens. There must be some part of the quality of our connection that has to do with me and my attitude, a part I haven't identified yet. But I sure can identify the part of our conflict that is in Dad's apparent inability to be loving and affirming to both Allen and me at the same time. His expressions of affection or condemnation toward

James and me when James was little were similar to this. James could do no wrong. I could do no right.

At bedtime last night, Dad thanked me (and Allen by proxy) for making what he called his "comfortable lifestyle here at home." I am glad, very glad, that he recognizes this, instead of being resentful about losing his autonomy and independence, complaining about having a cat that prefers me to him, or trying to refuse to spend money for a respite caregiver—all things that were issues when we started this gig. Progress!

This morning's AA meeting delivered to me the following wonderful phrase from the Alcoholics Anonymous "Big Book": "Cling to the thought that, in God's hands, the dark past is the greatest possession you have—the key to life and happiness for others. With it you can avert death and misery for them."[1]

We tell our stories to one another over and over in twelve-step meetings from the first time we are asked to chair a meeting. We share them as the best way to offer any help at all to others—as an invitation to them to identify with what we are sharing, not as a giving of advice or admonition. As a writer, as a recovering person, as a student of theology and of the Bible, I am a storyteller. And as a chaplain, I have been a story listener and a story receiver—or in hospice chaplain Kerry Egan's wonderful phrase, a *story holder*.[2]

Years ago I realized that, if none of my poetry was ever published or even read by anyone but me, it was serving me well, as it provided me with such an intricate and well-developed record of my own life that all the events, emotions, landscapes, people, and animals I described remained accessible to me. Now I can see that my poems also shape my recollections of these things. The narrative of the poetry has made the narrative of remembrance more alive. That is my wish with this record, which began last July in desperation as I considered who I was going to be now in the role of caregiver for my dad, without my job at the big hospital, with all the woundedness and the defeat, as well as the successes, of that time there. The mystery of that, with the new mystery of the end of my father's life imposed over it.

In examining those mysteries, I encounter the mystery of my own larger life—just what do I still want to do with my life? I had a massage the other day, and as I was drifting under the body worker's hands, listening

1. *Alcoholics Anonymous*, 124.
2. Egan, *On Living*, 17.

to the CD she had on of seagulls and waves and piano music, I thought that naming my experiences helps me recognize threads, patterns, progressions, regressions. And words are all I have, I'm not a painter or a musician; words, and the pictures and the music they can make.

***

Why is it hard for me to write in here when things happen with Dad's body that make awareness of his actual mortality so overwhelming? I am aware of how tired thinking about his death makes me, how sad, and how difficult everything can seem. It was hard to go to my new volunteer work as the palliative care chaplain at a small local hospital today, and it was hard to go on to James and Emily's house afterward. I felt afraid. Afraid Dad would die, and anxious because I had wasted all this time in being cross and overwhelmed, all these months and years . . . but then, I felt renewed by being away. Renewed or distracted? I can't tell. I remember when my mother was dying that wherever I was felt like the wrong place—when I was with her, I felt I should be at work, when I was at work, I felt I should be with her. Maybe there is just *no way* to do this "right." And there is the perennial temptation, for me, to feel that being a witness to, a handmaiden to, *Dad's* life, is somehow more important than living *my own life*.

Despair.

And all day he has been having troubles with his bathroom functions, which he will never describe clearly, but which has made him more and more cross as the day goes on, and I realize that some of my own irritability and prickliness is defensively designed to keep him and *his* irritability and prickliness at a distance. Now I am in the position, yet again, of feeling I ought to be gentler and more attentive and soak up every fleeting moment at the same time that I am trying to keep my head down and keep him at bay.

Like my childhood—"Don't let Daddy know how much I had to drink." And, simultaneously—"Don't let Mommy have any more to drink." Contain two impossible opposites.

10

The Gift of Limitation

> John 9:4:
> We must work the works of him who sent me while it is day; night is coming when no one can work.
>
> John 13:21–30:
> After saying this, Jesus was troubled in spirit, and declared, "Very truly, I tell you, one of you will betray me." The disciples looked at one another, uncertain of whom he was speaking. One of his disciples—the one whom Jesus loved—was reclining next to him; Simon Peter therefore motioned to him to ask Jesus of whom he was speaking. So while reclining next to Jesus, he asked him, "Lord, who is it?" Jesus answered, "It is the one to whom I give this piece of bread when I have dipped it in the dish." So when he had dipped the piece of bread, he gave it to Judas son of Simon Iscariot. After he received the piece of bread, Satan entered into him. Jesus said to him, "Do quickly what you are going to do." Now no one at the table knew why he said this to him. Some thought that, because Judas had the common purse, Jesus was telling him, "Buy what we need for the festival"; or, that he should give something to the poor. So, after receiving the piece of bread, he immediately went out. And it was night.

THE NIGHT WHICH BEGINS when Judas leaves is a particular kind of night. In John's Gospel, the word *night* refers not so much to a time of day as it

The Gift of Limitation

does to deep spiritual darkness. Judas has gone out to set in motion the events that will end Jesus's life; therefore, it is night.[1]

Before I made peace with Christianity as an expression of human spirituality, I spent a lot of time reading works from Eastern religions in a way that makes me cringe now, as I was so presumptuous in my appropriation of others' traditions and understandings. *I Ching* was one I read over and over. Hexagram 60 of *I Ching* is Limitation, which fleshes out the concept that it is the existence of limits which gives form, shape, and meaning to anything.[2] Over the years, as I have thought about this, I have combined *I Ching* and John's Gospel to conclude that limitations of light, of work, of life are good, not bad. Night or darkness represent conclusion but not evil.

Limitations provide meaning or, at least, an incentive to look for or create meaning. These ideas of limitation, of separation, of conclusion, play out in human thinking over and over. We have to come to terms with the limitations of our lives somehow.

The theology I make from the accounts of Jesus's crucifixion, the ending of his life on earth, is not a theology of preplanned, atoning, scapegoat sacrifice; not the end of light, and evil entering into the world. The theology I make is a teaching about limitation. A metaphor that tells me God joins me in even this, even in limitation. It illustrates the truth that God is present everywhere, even in endings we don't want. In the limitations imposed on creation by mortality. Night comes to end Jesus's work before it is through, just as my work will be ended before it is through. And this is part of God's good creation, this business of ending, of dying, for by it the earth will not be overrun. Awareness of our limitations also offers us the incentive to improve whatever we can about our own lives, and the lives of others—for time is short—and to savor what is good already.

Limitations to possibility. "Night is coming when no one can work." Limitations to our plans, but not to our hopes. And therefore, in the Christian story, we never stop with the crucifixion, with the ending of Jesus's life. We look ahead to the resurrection—a metaphor not of recurring cycles of rebirth, but of new life where there is no reason to expect it. Jesus died, his time on Planet Earth ended, his work as a young man so long ago is over, but his Work has not ended. Just as our work may live on after us, in ways we cannot control or foresee.

---

1. Bultmann, *Gospel of John*, 483.
2. *I Ching*, 231–34.

A Matter of Death and Life

***

In the midst of his dying (and mine, too), my dad and I sit at the kitchen table and he eats a peanut butter and jelly sandwich, which is easier for him to swallow than water is, and we talk about the snow and the rain and the ice and the clouds. All the February weather. He says he prefers the nice clean look of fresh snow to the bare gray ground, and I say I do too.

Today is the twenty-first anniversary of my mom's death and the 107th anniversary of her birth. I was in a terrible mood when I got up, which lasted until after lunch. Then I began slowly to feel better, maybe because yet another rain/snow/ice/melt/freeze/wind thing has turned to sun, even though it is now very cold. Maybe because I just hunkered down and didn't try to do much except "be" this morning. Maybe because my dad's hospice volunteer came to visit with him, and Allen and I went to the post office and the library together. Maybe because of lunch! Which included two Orange Milano cookies, which I scolded Allen heartily for buying the other day. The damn things have distracted me all week . . . bah!

Food addiction sucks. It's my hardest addiction in terms of having to pay attention to constant managing and feeling lost about how to do it. I knew it would be hard when I was back here in Dad's house, with his snack food larder, and I have actually done very well given that during six years of living alone in southern Maine I could control the level of my stimulation from comfort food by not having it around. This house, in contrast, is awash in chocolate, ice cream, bread and butter, crackers, and cookies.

Allen and I work separately, and sometimes together, to set boundaries on my dad's neediness. *Neediness* as opposed to *need*. I hate to think that someday my son will feel this way about me; I hope so much that I can be a different person in my dying time, my death, a nondemanding person. Yet who can really be nondemanding when faced with the blotting out of everything, heading off into the unknowable unknown, forever?

With my mom, both Allen and I had some amazing conversations about death. I could say to her, "I can't imagine what it will be like when you are gone." And she could say, "Me either." But I can't sidle up to that topic in conversation with my dad.

***

I am reading *The Doomsday Machine* by Daniel Ellsberg. Hard not to be depressed by it. It doesn't surprise me to learn how vicious the war planners were during World War II, World War I, and the Civil War—or really, during any war. It's not new information to read of the effects of the firebombing of Hamburg or Dresden or Tokyo; it's not new information to read about the ideas and the plans of military generals. But it is overwhelming to see Ellsberg's account of all of this, and more, assembled by him so lucidly, with such detail. It is very hard not to think we could flounder our way into nuclear war quite easily.

John Kennedy was a more restrained and ethical person than some presidents we have had, but he wasn't the one truly in control during the Cuban Missile Crisis in October 1962, a thirteen-day standoff during which disaster was avoided by a series of fortunate small decisions more than by JFK's actions or Bobby Kennedy's or Khrushchev's, even though they were actually trying to do the right thing. (After allowing the whole mess to get started in the first place.) Combining Ellsberg's pointed awareness of nuclear proliferation, political agendas, and bellicosity with our increasing awareness of the facts of climate change and my own awareness of death as I walk beside my father—it's a lot. Once I have finished this book, I probably need to find something less ominous to read.

I didn't feel as if I could muster the enthusiasm to lead worship this morning at the church Allen and I serve, although it was my turn, but as with other things I do that are not part of dad-care, I felt better once I left the house and got involved in doing my job, being with other people, and thinking about other things. And I have been able to feel tenderness toward my dad today. I finally convinced him to take a shower and to let me wash his hair and his back. We only do this about once every six weeks, and it takes a lot out of him, but these basics have to happen. I think. It is one of the many things I struggle over—*am I being controlling or am I right that this is part of maintaining basic health—avoiding skin irritation, basically keeping his skin healthy?* I see my gradual taking on of more and more tasks, a very slow process that involves first helping him with something, then doing it myself or asking Allen to do it. We've done this with food, with laundry, with hygiene, with paying bills, with getting library books, with birthday cards for friends and family, and so on. I try to pay attention to whether I am adding things but not letting go of things—in other words, accepting my own limitations . . .

I need to maintain my sobriety and my abstinence with food. I need to maintain my friendships and do housework, get exercise, help plan Allen's and my financial future, do my job at the church and my volunteer work, and so much more. I think I will know if the time comes when I have to let go of more in order to do the dad-thing. But I'd better pay good attention.

***

After a small crisis I found some financial papers Dad couldn't find. Interestingly, they were with *my* papers, which makes me think that I probably sequestered them there a while ago because he was going to throw them away, which he also does with paid bills. The lesson learned by me, though, is that I should file them in the filing system he started years ago even though he never uses it anymore. If they're in the filing cabinet, then I can at least find them. I probably did intend to do that when I put them with my stuff but then I lost track.

I think Dad and I will be in this weird zone for a while where I don't really want to take on managing his finances but I can't really trust him to keep up with it as he always has. I don't want the additional headache of adding more items to the stuff I am already doing, and I don't want to take something away from him that he can still do. I think that would be disrespectful of his adult autonomy and it would make him feel bad. But can he still do it?

We did get to a calm and connected place once I found the papers, and had a nice, mature conversation about Allen's and my financial future. But then Dad seemed sad. I don't know if that is because talking about the future is really also talking about the way it will be when he is dead. Or maybe he isn't sad at all. Maybe I am the one who is sad and I am projecting that emotion onto him. He may just be tired. Because, after all, he is dying. As am I, although I am a good deal more robust than he is at this point. It felt really good, though, both to have found the papers and to have the calm conversation. I felt loving and loved.

But, I still don't want to have a conversation with Dad about his dying. Not only do we have a very different relationship from the one I had with my mom, I am a very different person from who I was twenty-one years ago when she was dying. Since then, I've heard many, many stories from people about dying—told by the central figure in the drama, the soon-to-be-deceased, by their families, by their friends, by their medical caregivers, and by other chaplains. My own death is twenty-one years closer to me than it was. And I am less cocooned by my various addictions.

In addition, my mother's cancer diagnosis gave her a reasonably clear timeline for her dying, whereas my dad could go on for years—a span that makes preserving our psychic distance, even in the increasing intimacy of my caregiving for him, very important as a way of maintaining my own sense of self. I don't want to think about his death in its existential magnificence. I want to think about *me*.

When my dad goes, all that will be left of my original family will be me. All the memories and stories and artifacts will be mine alone. I feel so often that I am keeping myself held in a thin wrapping—holding back from Dad not because of what he is demanding or might demand of me but because of what I am *afraid* he might demand. I fear what his very beingness might demand. Clearly, I'm describing an interior state of mine, not an exterior state of his. I feel such a need to keep him at arm's length.

One really stunning thing recently, as I helped Dad pay bills and balance his checkbook, was the realization that Dad alive is part of Allen's and my income. He receives decent Social Security and gets a break on his property taxes because he is a veteran. Both of those things will cease when he dies. We benefit from both of those things. Dad's income supports his house in which we live with him. He pays the taxes, for example. Yes, I will inherit whatever remains of his money when he dies. But I won't inherit his Social Security and I won't inherit his property tax break.

That realization made me more deeply aware that I can and must do more self-care *now*. Him dying won't guarantee my ability to take care of myself, and resenting him for being alive is not the way I want to live. And focusing on my needs for self-care and my right to live *my* life rather than subsume all that to his puts me in touch with the actual deep love I feel for him.

Yesterday I spent the morning participating in a presentation about advanced directives made by the palliative care team at the small hospital. As I have observed before, and can't believe that I still so easily forget, as soon as I oozed my way into being out there in the world, I felt differently from how I had been feeling when at home with Dad—not exactly happy, but grounded differently.

But, he was very cross with me when I got home and I wouldn't cater to him. He wanted me to bring my computer into the living room and work there beside him, which I have sometimes done, but not often, as he talks to me or turns on the television. I said no, I need to be up in my office.

"Why?"

"Because I need my desk."

I was glad I didn't bite his head off even though I wanted to say, "Because it's my life and I want to work in my office, that's why." He proceeded throughout the evening to pick at me about little things—even saying, "Why are you standing up so often?" (I came and went from the living room couch a few times during his news show.)

He was even more cross when I told him that today I am going to Orono to babysit the grandkids and I will be there overnight. I could feel emerging in me a twinge of guilt about not being attentive enough to him, some anger about feeling guilty, and a need to deconstruct the situation and see that, in reality, his happiness is not my problem to solve as much as I do genuinely want him to be happy. He was cross and negative, but at bedtime he apologized and took responsibility for being a "crabby old man." And I felt compassion. But was not tempted to change my plans.

I did not feel that his happiness was more important than mine last night.

I am going to stop writing for now, and go fix his breakfast, because he needs breakfast and can't do it for himself anymore. But I can't give up everything. And I won't.

***

It struck me this morning, reflecting on yesterday, that the last two times Dad has had a bad spell we have essentially given him palliative care. We've not taken him to the emergency room when he first brings it up, but instead helped him think things through (we did this several times yesterday) and make the decision to just stay home. I know he doesn't want heroic measures if his heart stops, but he has always loved going to the doctor and being told that all his little aches and quirky sensations are "nothing to worry about." Doctors offer no big interventions, but a constant stream of small tweaks, which adds up to the same thing, in a way. This new approach is not as dramatic, not as costly as emergency room visits. It will also help us avoid a continual, fruitless involvement with the medical system—fruitless in the sense that there isn't anything to be done about the process of aging. Going forward, as the principal decision-maker for Dad, with lots of support and input from James and Allen and Dad's doctor, I am keeping him on the course that I think is what he actually wants—palliation with rest, fluids, easy-to-digest foods, Tylenol, and TUMS.

It occurs to me that folks without my understanding of end-of-life issues, my experiences in hospitals as one of the staff, or without the support system I have would probably be going to the emergency room multiple times, to have all sorts of things tested and scanned, and then go home even more tired and with no diagnosis and no magic pills, because there isn't anything "wrong" for medical intervention to fix. What is wrong is corrected by comfort measures.

From my years as a chaplain in various medical environments, I know some general things, and one of them is that doctors often aren't clear enough with people who are dying. I don't think Dad is actively and immediately dying, but he is in the dying process, whatever that will mean for him. He has a wonderful, trusting relationship with his doctor that goes back many, many years and the doctor is warm and caring and competent and kind, all of which is beneficial. But I wonder whether a palliative care doctor would have a franker conversation with Dad about the changes in his body. Maybe I am completely wrong, but I wonder.

I don't really think there is any care that we are not providing that should be provided, but I wonder whether the doctor could talk about aging and dying with Dad in a way I can't. I do think I could talk about that very thing with the doctor myself, though, and maybe this realization will inspire me to do so. But for now, it falls under the heading of "things that feel like one more exhausting thing to do."

His doctor did suggest a bottle of prescription-strength cough medicine with codeine in it to possibly ease Dad's constant nighttime coughing. I gave Dad one teaspoonful in the afternoon as a test to see how it might affect his balance or if it would cause other unwanted side effects. It seemed to work fine and it did inhibit the coughing. I gave him another teaspoonful at bedtime. He is still asleep this morning but seems to have had a good night. Now I have some questions about where this goes. *Do we give him codeine every night?* Because the coughing is not going to get better. He will get habituated to the cough medicine, we will need more and more, it isn't paid for by insurance, it can't be a long-term solution, etc., etc. *So, what is the point?* It's like giving sleeping pills to someone with lifelong poor sleep. *If you sleep poorly almost every night why bother ever taking a pill, because you will really have to take it forever . . .*

Scratch all that about the "good night" and the possible love affair with, and commitment to, codeine. Dad just woke up and said how awful he feels—completely washed out. I told him, and I think this is true, that being logy is at least partly from the codeine. But I feel at an impasse about where we are and what to do next. Maybe I, too, have hopes of a "something" that would make it better.

When I asked the doctor for a swallow study for Dad last summer, the therapist identified "pooling" (mild) and made suggestions about positional changes when swallowing, or icy cold liquids, or ginger ale. To date, Dad hasn't been willing to do any of it. He was always pretty compliant with things like food regimens and exercising for health purposes, but he was also always pretty healthy, in fact very heathy, without having to do much. It is different to be compliant when you have to work hard at it.

I don't understand the mechanisms of swallowing well enough, and I am wary of making false correlations and assumptions, but it seems to me that Dad's violent coughing when he swallows liquid—water most of all—is the clue that his general coughing has to do with managing his secretions. I am discouraged. Not because there isn't a cure, but because I thought maybe with the codeine we had hit on a comfort measure.

* * *

I decided to ask his doctor if Dad could be referred to hospice now, if he would qualify, which he did not last summer. When I was the hospice chaplain, folks could be admitted for old age, essentially, if their function was low enough and their decline could be regularly documented. The doctor agreed with me that he is at a lower level than he was. And he agreed that it might be an appropriate referral, suggesting home health services as well, as an alternative. If he would qualify for this kind of care, that would be a fine place to start. I just want there to be someone knowledgeable checking in on him regularly. I feel pretty smart about what I see, but I'm not so smart that I don't need support and guidance. And I am not objective at all. We just went through ten or so exhausting days of Dad having poor sleep, complaining a lot about the coughing and his general feeling of malaise, and I want to do something to make him more comfortable if that is possible. This stage of his dying is still very easy compared to how it could be, but I want to be proactive, for my sake as well as his, if there is anything proactive we can do.

The doctor suggested that he would investigate which would be quicker to get in place—home health or hospice. I said that whatever was decided about hospice, my dad would have to agree, have to be part of the decision, and so the doctor backtracked a bit and said, "Good point." I feel like I can be too aggressive and too "take charge," but this was an example of me really wanting to respect my dad's autonomy and decision-making powers. This is his life we are talking about. I am very clear that he does not want—and we would not want to convince him of a need for—aggressive treatment. But I think the idea of hospice will unfortunately be dismaying to him, which is true for so many folks, and that is too bad as so many folks would benefit from that approach to end-of-life care.

You can be admitted to hospice, which in our part of the world means being cared for at home, mostly by your family; and get a lot of really good, really focused care and "graduate" from hospice (i.e., stop qualifying for services) because you aren't declining any longer! I would want to present this option very carefully. If he could start with home health care that would be best perhaps.

11

Negative Space

AWAITING THE FIRST VISIT of the home health nurse. In preparation, Allen and I have tried to review the last two weeks with Dad, but he doesn't remember any of them. He feels reasonably well right now, so he thinks he has felt reasonably well for the whole time period; although when I remind him, he can agree that he felt awful last weekend. I have often heard said of a patient with many medical issues, including those at the beginning of dementia, "He has no insight into his illness." That expression seems to apply to Dad at this point in time: he has no insight into, or more likely doesn't want to have insight into, his aging process. (Thankfully, he is showing no signs of dementia.)

Dad doesn't want it to be true that he is in a phase of life unlike all the other phases of life: the ending phase. He comments over and over that he doesn't want to be a burden, which only brings us to an impasse. He can't keep in focus that he has no choice about this, that he *is* a burden in the sense of needing much care and attention. But, we are choosing this path with him out of love, so it is not "burdensome."

I am clearly the emotional center of my dad's life now, and perhaps always have been. I am not the emotional center in the sense of being a sparkling, spicy distraction, but I am the emotional center in the sense of being the one who mediates the basics of his existence. I don't just mean that I am (now) in charge of commode, Depends, clean clothes and linens, interesting food, and so on. I mean that I am the steady energy force that provides emotional accompaniment to his days.

When I was younger, a little girl, I think I *was* the sparkling, spicy distraction. But then I got older and my mother brought me over to her side, so to speak, and I began to drink like her and break rules. I don't think he could have accepted my differentiation well in any case, because he hasn't been very successful in self-directed efforts to manage his own anxiety and sadness, and so he wanted me, as one wants a commodity, to be an extension of him, in a sense, to pull him out of that state. And, in a sense, to mother him.

The night before last, Dad had a terrible night of coughing according to him, and I believe that that was his perception. Although Allen and I often hear him in the night, and while I heard more coughing than sometimes, I didn't hear it "all night." Anyway, yesterday morning he felt awful and, as usual, felt like this was something new. I always feel perplexed by this and wonder: *Is it better, as with an identified dementia patient, not to argue, or better to talk him out of it, as I have done all my life with him?* I generally take the second course and feel like an emotional bully, which is what happened yesterday.

"Yes, you've had this before," I said. "Yes, the doctor has checked it out. Yes, there is nothing wrong with you that they can treat."

Fortunately, the next night he had a good night with almost no coughing, and was able to agree with me that the coughing comes and goes, rather than insisting that something big is happening, something new and unique that must be addressed. He's had a decent day today as far as I can tell; the home health nurse came and again had no ideas about the coughing, but confirmed that his lungs were clear. He liked her and they had a good visit.

After the nurse left, Dad and I talked further and he said, "I know where this is headed. At age ninety-eight, you have to be a realist." He told me that the morning before he'd wanted to go to the ER but talked himself out of it. We got to have a nice, reality-based conversation affirming his desire to stay out of the hospital and have minimal medical interventions. So much better than the times when he says he wants to "check himself into the hospital" and other bizarre ideas. He may go back into the cloud of denial again, that may be how he will cope, or he may have come to terms with something. In any case, he feels better today than yesterday.

***

After two pretty decent days with Dad, yesterday was hard. He was anxious about money and fussing again about paying Mary to stay with him when Allen and I are away for several hours. He asked how much we pay her and was outraged when I told him twenty dollars an hour. And I quickly and angrily told him, "Don't go there again! An agency would charge you thirty dollars. This is the cheapest way for you to do this! You get a lot of free care from your family!" And he subsided. I don't know whether pushing back so forcefully is a good way to handle that ongoing issue. It goes away, it comes back. He sits there fussing over his checkbook like a caricature of a miser. Yet he is very generous with his financial gifts to us all.

But the worst of it was during the evening time when we always drug ourselves with the nightly news. He and I were having some difficulty communicating anyway as I discovered that his usual beloved PBS *NewsHour* wasn't on as this is the week of the Maine State Basketball Championships, which he hates and which every year since moving to Maine in 1986 he has complained about.

"I am sure there can't be many people who want to watch this!" he says.

And I think, but don't say, not wanting to inflame him—*no, Dad, you are wrong! Think of all the people who can't go to Augusta or Bangor to watch their beloved grandson or granddaughter play ball!*

I couldn't quite believe there wasn't some different time slot for the *NewsHour* and kept scanning the guide channel of the television set; due to his hearing and always slow comprehension of what I am doing with the television, he was a step or two behind me, asking me questions, complaining as I tried to concentrate and flip around among screens looking for a news program for him. Finally I settled on NBC and then *I* was interested in a brief segment on the upcoming winter storm and was explaining to him what I had done—Ah! Now we can watch this—and he chose that moment to mute the sound.

I snatched the remote back from him, turned up the volume, and said something sharp, which of course he could not hear although he got my tone of voice for sure. We had some further impatient interaction (impatient on my part) and he put his face in his hands, the way he does when he is just overwhelmed by feelings, usually frustration and hurt, which come to the surface in reaction to me only. And as I watched the brief news segment, I felt such shame, and also the pain of my own frustration and stuck-ness.

He said again at bedtime, "I know I am a burden." And I said then, "No, you are not, we love you." I said it again this morning and it is true, but also not true. The "love you" part is true, but the burden part is more complex. I am aware in a deeper way than I was able to be when this new level of caregiving began last summer, of how much I will miss him when he is gone, how inconceivable his being gone forever is—but this *is* a burden too.

* * *

The last time I met with my therapist, I was talking about my need to generate narrative about events in my life, my hunger to find or spin a thread that makes the evidently disparate parts cohere into something that adds up to Something. And I told my therapist that in real life, unlike in good fiction, sometimes the bits don't cohere very well. Sometimes there are plot threads that don't fit into the weave. In a novel, a good editor would throw those out. Life has to contain them, though. Real life doesn't have to be consistent or convincing or coherent. It often isn't any of these things, it just is.

My therapist proposed a metaphor from psychotherapy—a stained-glass window with lots of bits of colored glass held together by leading. She said that some pieces will have sharp edges, requiring caution, but they need to be included and held together in a whole with the other pieces. I appreciate the image of life as stained glass, with all the bits and pieces held together and letting the light through. Letting light through, in different strengths and in different colors.

A picture flashes past on my laptop's screen saver as I pause to think—the mantelpiece of the place where I house-sat for three winters during my time as chaplain at the big hospital, a picture of the little white lights I strung along its edge, with figures from my childhood Christmases replacing the knickknacks of the folks whose home it was. Seeing that little picture reminds me of how lonely I was there, and yet, of how I made that place, that life, my own in so many ways. And then the next picture comes on the screen saver, this time grandson Jack and Allen in the kitchen of James and Emily's house a few years ago, and I see how the screen saver is an even more accurate metaphor, perhaps, than a stained-glass window or the threads of a narrative tapestry—because the pictures are not in order, they just come as they come, and it is mind, memory work, that makes them into more than just pixels—locations—imbued with light.

It is snowing still, after a blizzard all night. Dad was discharged from home health services yesterday after only two weeks, two weeks in which nothing went wrong except for a bout of diarrhea, which was not related to anything new. He's too healthy to qualify.

12

Another Turn of the Wheel

DAD STARTED COUGHING AGAIN, a lot. Called me in the night because he was cold and wanted a blanket. He felt very warm to the touch, accepted some cough medicine, declined Tylenol. Later, I felt his face as he dozed, and this time woke him up enough to insist he take some. Allen helped him to the commode, as he was floppy. Allen slept in the big chair downstairs in case he needed help again. In my own not-very-deep sleep all night, I realized that if/when we get to the part of this where my father is truly and mostly suffering, it is going to be very hard for me. Different from how it was with my mom. I am different, the relationship I have with my dad is different, but mostly, he is different from her. When Dad is feeling really bad, he is like a bewildered little child. Mom was stoic, angry, philosophical, and had a lot of bravado. He projects the child's hope that if he can behave well enough, be good enough, it will go away.

***

I am in a really, really bad place. I woke up too early, as so often. My dad has evidently totally recovered. Hard for me not to feel bitter and put upon and annoyed by the whole thing. He did genuinely have a fever and chills and almost constant coughing Sunday night, but by the time a home health nurse came on Monday, he was already better.

It's just another turn of the wheel. I feel such rage! Which is why I better just shut the hell up. This doesn't seem like a "live and thrive" message to my interior Little Girl. "Shut the hell up" is not loving. But it seems as if being honest with everyone about how much I want, how much I need, or what I demand will only make things worse. Other people are not responsible for my happiness.

Isn't the rage really about the entrapment that I feel? The sense of being sentenced to take care of my father indefinitely? This feeling of entrapment blends with the sheer incomprehensibility and loss I also feel when I contemplate my father actually dying. I feel stuck in an eternal not-changingness in his care, and also afraid of the ending of this limbo because this limbo ends with the loss of him. I am depressed, very depressed, about how I will make a life without him in it. With the illogic of the state I am in, I feel abandonment, and pointlessness, lovelessness, and futility.

***

We are waiting for snow. Last week we had a good foot and a half, today another twenty inches or so is expected. Dull gray sky, silent and still gray trees, the white of last week's storm absorbing the blank light of dawn. Sullen. Opaque. I, too, am opaque, sullen, brooding, perhaps like the snow-sodden landscape, unable to imagine light. Cannot imagine a break from myself, freedom from this trap of caring and being hurt.

My father awakens in the next room and begins his coughing. I sit hoping to hear his breathing drift back into its sleep rhythm, but instead hear the little noises of his bed as he sits up.

***

Breakfast conversation with Dad, who asks if I have spoken with the doctor.

Him: I certainly don't want any antibiotics.

Me: Even if the doctor recommends them, based on the nurses' report? What about if you have a fever again tonight? Would you want them then?

Him: I am not sure.

Me: This is important, Dad. I definitely support you having or not having them, it's your choice. But when you don't feel well, you often say you want to go to the hospital. There they would surely give you antibiotics if they admitted you. Antibiotics could be life-saving, or they could be what prevented you from having a peaceful, natural death. I need guidance from you about what you want.

Him: I want to live to be a hundred.

Me: At any price? Or only if you have a reasonable quality of life?

Him: (reluctantly) Only if I have a reasonable quality of life.

I suppose it isn't unreasonable for me to dread the idea of Dad lasting to one hundred, but I feel guilty that rather than thinking, *Yay! My parent wants to keep on! What a pip! More power to him*, I feel dread. I want so much for him to die without too much distress for either of us and it is very hard to imagine how we get through the fifteen more months until his hundredth birthday. And what happens then anyway?

Of course, of course, this process with my dad can only be done one day at a time. Allen and I probably need to figure out more respite for ourselves, together.

This is why I don't believe in "Advance Directives." My father filled one out long ago, when he was "young." The last time it was updated was thirteen years ago. It covers, with broad strokes, actual end-of-life care decisions. As a result, he probably won't end up costing his insurance company thousands of dollars while he languishes in an intensive care unit. But the last round of our conversation about the antibiotics was him saying, "I don't want to be billed for something I don't want." Back to money again. His chief anxiety. And anything I tried to say, very patiently with a gentle voice, about "Do you or don't you want medical interventions? And if you aren't willing to follow the advice doctors would give you, we don't want to involve them fruitlessly" he deflected.

Him: I feel fine now.

Me: That is the best time to talk about this—not during a crisis, but when you feel fine.

Ultimately, I did get impatient when he interrupted my carefully chosen words to say that the cat needed more treats. So much for having The Conversation.

***

Yesterday Dad said, "Sometimes I get depressed."

I said—and this was said with a caring feeling in my heart and in my voice—"You have been depressed your whole life, I think, off and on."

And he said, "Yes, I think you are right."

I said, "I think the best thing for you to do is distract yourself." Which is surely not what I would say to most people; rather, I would be advocating for working on their underlying issues. But how do you do that when you are ninety-eight and probably haven't begun?

I said caring things, I think, reassuring him about our commitment to him, our love for him. But what I didn't say was, "Are you worrying about death?" Maybe I will try saying that today somehow. But I don't want to go there with him, I am his daughter, not his chaplain. It feels like such a dark space, a black hole.

While we talk, I can imagine myself about to be different, more compassionate, less impatient, something—but as the interaction goes streaming by, I don't do anything different from the last time we had it. My dad does not talk about depression with Allen, only about windows and other household maintenance projects. It is I alone with whom he has the truly vulnerable conversations—vulnerable but not quite tipping his hand, not quite revealing what is really going on inside of him, which means I can play along and we stay on the surface.

Is that what he really wants? Just to be reassured? I don't feel like I have the energy to delicately tease out a deeper conversation. Best just to let sleeping dogs lie. Or something. Will I regret this when he is gone?

I would like it if I understood my own motivations better. I can see vaguely that it is hard to keep an eye on how Dad is doing while not invading his privacy, while also taking care of the parts of his life that he has relinquished, and to also have the leisure to be a daughter who engages in conversations about memories or the world scene or his depression. I don't have the energy for all of it, but I suspect that some of the lack of energy is within me, not just within the situation, and that is the part I want to understand better. What am I fending off, in myself, with this psychic inertia?

Later yesterday, because we had been communicating well, I took the risk of asking Dad, carefully, if his feeling depressed was at all in relation to "contemplating his demise." I got that phrasing from a long-ago hospice patient—euphemistic, but also, with someone like that man long ago and my dad, appropriate. Appropriate for a generation that lives its entire emotional life in euphemisms. This is the generation that puts the word *fondly* or *affectionately* instead of *love* before the signature as the closing for a letter. "Put out" rather than "angry." "Out of sorts" rather than "sad."

A while ago I started saying "I love you" to my dad at bedtime and now he usually says it back, a very unusual thing in the culture of our family.

But Dad emphatically denied any thoughts about death with a quick, unadorned "no." He didn't even crack the door with a "maybe" or a "possibly." Just "no." Unsaid were possibilities like "I am not depressed about my demise because I am not thinking about or acknowledging any feelings I have about my death and its likely nearness."

And then he proceeded to have a good day, as far as I could tell.

***

My work as a chaplain, and my time as a daughter to my dying mother and now to my declining dad, makes me very aware of how much most people want company as they approach their own fearsome and incomprehensible death—the end of being as we know it, or so it is logical to assume, despite any hope one might have for bodily resurrection or life in heaven and so forth. In the biblical accounts, even Jesus actually *dies*, actually stops being "himself." The deepest, oldest, truest meaning of Jesus's resurrection is not a restoration to life as it had been for him, for his followers, for anyone, but a new and previously inconceivable state of being. If there is anything like that in store for us *Homo sapiens sapiens*, it is not something we can know ahead of time, although we may have philosophies, beliefs, faith statements about it—but there is no experiential, empirical knowledge about what happens after we die.

It is possible to think of aging itself as a kind of illness, although generally speaking I would not do so, for I believe that it is a natural process and not something to be cured. But with aging comes so much change, so much loss, and like my dad, I am afraid of losing my mind, or at least its acuity, I am afraid of losing my body's stamina, strength, and flexibility—which is actually already happening. I am afraid of losing my husband and my friends as they age at a different rate from me. Even more terrifying and unthinkable are the losses of children and grandchildren that may accompany long lives. And I acknowledge that the insecurities of my childhood, plus the role modeling of my dad and his family with their legacy of perpetual anxiety, have made me afraid throughout my whole life thus far of losing these attachments. Losing them without even losing them, in the sense of feeling abandoned due to my parents' limited abilities to be present with me when I was small; of feeling unlovable.

In my experience, there are folks who avoid meaning-making about their lives or the life of the universe, etc., as much as possible, because to engage in it can be such a vulnerable activity. There are folks whose meaning-making remains insistently on the level of the material, centering on issues of wealth, status, appearances, possessions, indulgence of addictions. But we all do die, whether or not we are thoughtfully ready to do so. And it is true that many, many folks who want to live well understand that they have to come to terms with death and do that in a way that we could categorize under the heading of spirituality.

So, even though I am a Christian minister, I think of myself as an agnostic in the holiest sense of that word. It feels blasphemous to say anything about "God" definitively. But I do believe that there is a Power Greater Than Myself. And this I know "experimentally," in George Fox's wonderful phrase about his experience of the transcendent, which was, for him, expressed in traditional Christian terms, yet not quite in the traditional way:

> And when all my hopes in them and in all men were gone, so that I had nothing outwardly to help me, nor could tell what to do, then, Oh then, I heard a voice which said, "There is one, even Christ Jesus, that can speak to thy condition," and when I heard it my heart did leap for joy. Then the Lord did let me see why there was none upon the earth that could speak to my condition, namely, that I might give him all the glory; for all are concluded under sin, and shut up in unbelief as I had been, that Jesus Christ might have the preeminence, who enlightens, and gives grace, and faith, and power. Thus, when God doth work who shall prevent it? And this I knew experimentally.[1]

I shared with my therapist what Mary shared with me, that the work I did on separation and autonomy, triggered by some of my disappointments and losses in key relationships at the big hospital, she, Mary, did when her beloved cat Finch disappeared last fall. That event tore the scab off her wounds of childhood insecurity and loss. My therapist told me that, yes, this work can happen with any kind of relationship: with other people, with pets, even with objects.

So, there is my dad with his fears about the ongoing stewardship of familial possessions. "Always use a coaster" and "Keep sunlight from fading pictures and furniture" are almost the only hard and fast rules I can remember from childhood. The consolations of my father's attachments are housed in those possessions, the keeping of which, in some cases, goes back two hundred and fifty years. He passionately wants to see the family traditions of keeping or careful disposition of these things go forward. But I have

---

1. Fox, "Gathered People."

a love/hate relationship with them since they have always seemed more valuable to him than I myself am. In a sense, this is actually true, and also somewhat fortunate, because it has meant that despite that extreme projection of his need onto me, the Things are getting even more of it. Thank God. His spirituality is a spirituality of family stuff, almost like animism. I have a good dose of this too, in my reluctance to throw away his, mine, or James's old stuffed animals.

A hugely important aspect of positive attachment in my own life is the community I have found all these years in twelve-step program meetings. A key place for encountering a "Power Greater Than Myself." My challenge is to see that Power extending beyond those rooms, where I know it fleshed out in other people, incarnate if you will; and into the vast universe and the "place," if it is a place, where I will go alone when I die. As did my mom, mysteriously drawing her last breath, mysteriously becoming completely, completely still, for the very first time in her entire life on earth, since that first breath, that first squirm as a newborn. As will my dad. Only mysterious because it is a place we the living cannot, cannot go.

13

My Own Companion on the Journey

THERE ARE RESEARCH STUDIES that correlate health and church attendance, health and prayer, health and religious practice. But my guess is that what is actually good for one's health, what contributes to healing, is interaction and the perception on the part of the participants that interaction represents attentive caring. Which it may or may not; I know quite well from my professional life that one can be sad, tired, and distracted and still present a compassionate presence. The healing is not in the healer but in the act of presence itself. The caregiver does not have to be pure and faultless for their care to be effective.

***

In the spiritual care department of a hospital, as in a hospital generally, there is much talk about "coverage": covering the floors, covering the patients, covering the staff, covering the nights and the weekends. Chaplains want to see everyone, to serve everyone, at all times. But unlike the medical staff, the chaplains will not see everyone. There are never enough chaplains. We fret over coverage, over patients who go unseen.

There is not really a way to be efficient while making spiritual care visits. Thankfully. Thankfully, because the human economy of efficiency, and the divine economy of effectiveness are so often so very different. We read about Jesus's journey from Galilee to Jerusalem as it is told in all four

Gospels, particularly in John where it loops back and forth between places, almost without noticing that Jesus's path seems to be meandering and random. Even though their itineraries and timelines vary, none of the Gospel writers ever say that Jesus sat down with the disciples to draw up a plan for coverage, for prioritization of need, for maximum benefit for their efforts. One day Jesus teaches a crowd, heals many, or feeds five thousand people, but another day he is off to eat with a single person in their home. He spends far more time alone praying than most busy chaplains and ministers do. He knows that the whole world is his responsibility, and because of his inner clarity he can respond "immediately," Mark's chosen word for Jesus's actions, over and over again—yet Jesus never seems to be in a hurry.

Coverage can mean breadth—there are five thousand hungry people here, let's get them some food! (And, of course, Jesus didn't insist on handing out all the food himself: on the contrary, he told the disciples to do it.) Or it can mean depth—here is one person with a really important question that they are almost afraid to ask, let's make a space for them to articulate their deepest spiritual need. Ideally, of course, in terms of chaplaincy services, coverage would mean both breadth and depth. Everyone who wants to be seen by the chaplain would be seen, and each encounter would last long enough to get to the level of intimacy where that deep spiritual need is not covered, but *uncovered*.

Ten minutes with a young couple of no church community whose toddler is very ill; a one-minute prayer, followed by brusque dismissal, with an angry son who wants the right words said over his mom but is not religious himself; a friendly "hello" to a woman who a nurse wants seen, but who clearly doesn't want a visit—these are one kind of opportunity for coverage.

An hour spent with a family making an agonizing decision about whether to withdraw life support from a beloved grandmother; five twenty-minute visits over five weeks with a wife while her husband fights for his life (and loses the battle) in the ICU; a follow-up conversation with a social worker who has asked for a chaplain for the troubled daughter of a patient—these are another kind of opportunity for coverage.

Both are important; if chaplains are visible, a presence in the hospital, then they can be more useful as a resource. The busy medical staff will think of them more often when a patient has an emotional or spiritual need, and the patients will be more aware that they don't have to leave their spiritual selves in the locker with their clothing when they enter the hospital system and change into medical gowns. But if we worry too much about the breadth of our coverage, if we structure our visits for speed rather than for depth, then what we are doing can begin to seem meaningless—we are delivering postcards from the church rather than participating with the patient, the family member, the staff person in the mysterious action of the spirit of God, the spirit which has all the time in the world.

***

In my eyes, there has always been a childlike quality to my dad. He never seemed like a true grown up to me in many ways, even when I was much younger. Too uncertain, too anxious, too battered around by trivialities. How did this man go all through basic training as a Marine in World War II and serve four years, not in combat but very near it, in the Quartermaster Corps, traveling through the Pacific and in the occupying forces in northern China at war's end? And he earned a living, sustained a marriage, had friends, had interests. But I have never been able to discern a philosophy of life in him. Just his anxiety about doing what others expected, what conventions demanded. Would that be termed extreme codependence? Or is he just a very private person? In any case, my codependence leaves me with the illusion that of all the deaths in the world, his is the one of which I must be the guardian. That somehow I *can* step over the threshold with him, get him settled in in the netherworld, and then—what? Go back to my own life and my own eventual death?

My mother clearly didn't want anyone messing with *her* journey. How well I remember the night, about two weeks before she died, when she pulled off her oxygen cannula, insisted on climbing out of the bed, and sat in a chair wild-eyed and panting—a night of "Shut up," "Leave me alone," "Go away," as Allen and I tried to soothe her. Finally she relaxed and said over and over, "It's going to be all right." And only then did she let us help her back to bed.

She would have preferred to stay alive. When she was told by the doctors, "We can't offer you anything, so sorry," she said to me, "but I wanted to live to be eighty-six." (She was then eighty-five and a half.) Not ninety-six or 106, just another six months. But she had to die. And during that night of panting and resistance, she let go and accepted what was happening—"It's going to be all right."

***

We had a visit from a dear cousin of mine, someone Dad has known since he and my mother were courting, and it was good. Dad really enjoyed it and was easier to be with—not sure if it was because having an observer meant he behaved better, in the sense of being less demanding, less imperious in his interruptions of me and of Allen too—or if it was because he was getting so much attention from my cousin that he needed less from me, so I could get more space. Perhaps both. He definitely did less of the demanding kind of interruption that I so hate—but I also had less of an agenda. I wasn't trying to write, I wasn't the one preparing the worship service for the coming Sunday, so I was less focused on matters of my own which weren't relevant to him.

My cousin wanted to hear Dad's stories and share hers. A good example of why it is so important to have an extended family support system for the caregiver of someone who is making their way toward their death. For the five days of her visit, I often got to quietly sit back and not interact with Dad. He had plenty of interaction and a reason to rise to the occasion and be his best self.

**

Yesterday was awful. But the good news is that I was able to keep it in house; in my head, i.e., not flail around angrily blaming others for my mood, or trying to get others to fix me. I was just so sad, all day. My therapy session gave me some ideas to work with. My therapist said that during childhood I developed (as any neglected child will try to do) such good strategies for managing without an adult to help me, that I now have a very hard time nurturing the needs of my inner child. She is walled off from my adult life. The very skill with which I succeeded in surviving is in my way now. Having learned not to need much support and love from a wiser, older guide—or, probably more accurately, to sublimate that need for help from another to my own inadequate (because immature) self-soothing and self-guidance—it is hard now to learn to allow myself to experience my own needs and then enlist support from others in a healthy way, or know how to help myself. I am just too accustomed to managing beautifully, on the surface, with the hungry wasteland inside of me going unaddressed. This makes sense to me; it explains why I can function so well as chaplain or mother or grandmother or wife or daughter or mentor or friend while feeling so bereft, so destitute. It explains why I feel so despairing. The little child is in an airtight box, cut off from food, from light, from anything; safe, but frozen. And I have such trouble letting her out.

I identify that, when my heart aches for Dad and his loneliness, it is also aching for me. Maybe most of all it is aching for me. Because I feel so raw and afraid and alone, it is very hard to bear the imagined aloneness and sorrow and fear of my dad.

***

Came across this, written by me at the big hospital in January 2016:

> Meaning: In times of crisis, people usually seek to discover causation—to seek an extrinsic meaning in the events occurring; in other words, a meaning that is objectively true rather than a subjective one. They think that finding causation and extrinsic meaning will make them feel better. Wanting to get a diagnosis, a reason for a physical illness, is one example of this, even though what may actually happen is that a person undergoing diagnostic testing doesn't feel better emotionally at all when they find out, for example, that they have a cancer for which there is no cure.
>
> Chaplains and doctors deal in life and death, which equals authority over extrinsic meaning/events in the eyes of patients.
>
> I deal in metaphysics and superstition with the very often non-religious people I serve as they seek extrinsic meaning, but my experiences lead me to believe that it is the formation of intrinsic meaning—drawn from relationships in the moment—that is the most helpful in life generally, in times of crisis and distress particularly.

That all still rings true for me, two years later. My experiences with some folks at that hospital make me also believe that our need for the sense of comfort which a transitional object[1] provides is so powerful that until we have done the developmental work which allows us to give that sense of comfort to ourselves, to be our own transitional object in a sense, we will seek it by projecting that comfort-giving power onto all kinds of other people, whether or not they are remotely capable of giving us much of anything at all. I have been doing this work in my own life for a very long time, trying to get myself to a place where I have a steady and reliable sense of

---

1. Winnicott, "Transitional Objects."

attachment to myself; to my own ability to nurture *me*. This *essential* work. And all of this work is brought to a crux by living within the walls of my dad's decline and my own expanded awareness of mortality as I age.

We deal with awareness of our death through our religions and our philosophies, with our religious and spiritual practices, with our relationships, with our addictions, and with our striving and our denial and our hubris. We are never really apart from it.

My experience as a companion to my dad in this time of his approaching death leads me to a deeper awareness of my fears of my own death, of ceasing to be, and of the seeming futility of life at all, since it always, always ends in death. The embracing of limitation. Or rather, more accurately, the struggle to accept limitation. The struggle to believe it is a good thing. Part of life; life-affirming, even.

14

"All things shall perish from under the sky..."

For some reason, the stuff about the big city hospital where I worked, and my leaving of it, is really up for me again—maybe just because it is getting closer to the anniversary of my last days there. Yesterday evening was probably the annual memorial service for the pediatric patients, which I led for five years. I thought of them all, the families I won't see again, the staff with whom I went through so much. Wondered how my replacement did with it.

> All things shall perish from under the sky.
> Music alone shall live,
> Music alone shall live,
> Music alone shall live,
> Never to die.
> —Traditional German folk song

***

Yesterday Dad and I had one of our skirmishes, this time about him wanting, yet again, to get rid of things so that I, Alice, "won't be burdened with having to do it." Other times when this has come up I have deflected it by saying, "No, you don't need more money at this point, and you like having your pictures, your furniture, your books around. What would be the value of selling them and denuding this house now?" But yesterday when he persisted, I got annoyed enough that I finally said, "If you really wanted not to burden me, you should have done this ten years ago. For me to do it now is even harder than to do it when you are gone, as now I am trying to keep up with making a home for you."

At least I didn't say, "You are a lot of work already, and that would just add to it." Which is what I felt. Instead, I expanded upon my first comment by saying, "To go to a book dealer, an antiques dealer, an art dealer would take time that I don't have. It is on me whether it happens now or later." We did have a constructive conversation about antique punch cups though. He was willing to let them go to the Ark Animal Shelter fundraiser.

Last Friday, after a week of afternoon headaches, I had a horrible attack of vertigo in the morning, complete with immobilizing nausea. Naturally, I assumed I had a brain tumor. I felt so horrible that I slept most of the day, even cancelling the therapy appointment to which I had been looking forward. Saturday I felt better; Allen and I finished up summer readiness chores at the cabin and then spent the afternoon there with James and Emily and the kids on a perfect early spring day. The plan was that Allen and I would head over to Bar Harbor to hear a concert that Mary was singing in and that they would have supper with Dad, then James would spend the night there as a prelude to a twenty-four-hour shift at a small local hospital. All well and good. I suggested to Dad that he could come with us to the cabin, that we could bring over a height-adjustable toilet seat for him since that is one of his concerns about being there. He declined. But maybe he felt left out anyway, because, when Allen and I came back full of good humor from our day, Dad lit into me about May 9 (this was May 4) and how he did not, did not, did *not* need Mary to be here while we went to Bangor as his gardening person would be here then.

I explained that Mary and the gardener have very different roles, that the gardener has previously said firmly that she doesn't want to do any driving or caretaking for him, that she is happy as his gardener, and that it wouldn't be fair to ask her for something different. Not to mention that she would be outside gardening, wouldn't be here until ten o'clock, and Allen and I would have to leave by 7:30 a.m., and so on. It got heated, he got really adamant and would not listen to me, and I wouldn't back down.

He knew, and was still remembering, that the reason we were going to Bangor was to complete the transfer of ownership of the cabin to James, an

"All things shall perish from under the sky..."

appointment that not only was an hour away, but had been difficult to get on everyone's calendar as it meant reconciling the lawyer's schedule, Allen's schedule, my schedule, James's schedule, Mary's schedule, Emily's schedule, the kids' schedule. He said, "You are bullying me!"

And I said, "No, *you* are bullying *me*!" I also said, "You want Allen and me to live our own lives and this arrangement is part of it. I can't go off to Bangor, an hour away, for an appointment that I can't easily leave, and not worry about you here alone."

I don't remember all that was said; he wouldn't back down, but I wouldn't either. It was a standoff. But Allen and I left for our concert, knowing that James and Emily would be at Dad's house shortly, and I was determined that this was going to be the way it was. I said to Allen, "It is like when we had to insist that he stop driving. We can't negotiate on this." I probably said that to Dad too.

Part of my anger was that, once again, our argument was about money. He didn't want to pay Mary and the gardener and the lawn-mowing folks. But I knew that he was probably also jealous that we had all been at the cabin without him, even though he made the decision not to go over there. And that he was probably jealous that Allen and I were going to have some time alone together, although that feeling would have been the least accessible to him of all his feelings, as it would freak him out to admit to himself how possessive of me he is and has always been. And probably most deeply of all, he doesn't want to be old and deaf and frail and close to death. He is far too mentally lively to be okay with how much of our activities he misses.

I called James, who was picking up pizzas, and said, "Here's what just happened—I don't expect you to get involved, but if Grandpa brings it up, I wanted you to have a heads up. Do you think I am being unreasonable?"

He said, "No, you are right, but it also isn't unreasonable that he doesn't like the idea that he has to have someone with him." James felt that this was a parallel to choosing palliative rather than curative care, in the sense that, yeah, if you want to be left alone, you can be, although you will die from it eventually (similar to a choice for no further treatment).

It was a hard struggle for me to let go of it all enough to enjoy the night out and the concert, but I managed. And talking to Mary about it briefly afterward and to Allen in the car helped, as did my conversation with James. And, I was really, really glad I had given James the heads up because, sure enough, Dad did say something to him: "Your mother thinks I shouldn't be here alone."

And James gave a perfect answer: "None of us think you should be here alone."

By morning, as I half suspected would be the case, Dad was very sorry and it had all blown over. And when we actually did go to our appointment in Bangor, he was glad for Mary's company, and glad to stay in bed until his usual time, and to have her here to help with breakfast, etc., and be good company until we got back at noon. I guess I can say that I handled it better than I once would have, both in standing my ground and in letting go of the angry, trapped feelings afterward. I definitely felt like I had to be very, very careful though—careful in how I interacted with him, not wanting to get too close so that I wouldn't fly off the handle.

Me saying, "No, *you* are bullying *me*," felt as significant as Nora closing the door on her husband in Henrik Ibsen's *A Doll's House*.

***

I had an amazing dream last night. I often dream about beaches, waves of different sizes, many quite large, and about skillfully navigating roads through water. I am never afraid in these dreams. This was a very long, complex dream of driving, getting to the beach—not a beach I know in my waking life, but the one I always visit in these dreams: a sandy beach with bathhouses and plenty of other bathers. A surf beach like the ones I went to with my mom and her sisters or with my mom and dad many times, or just my dad long, long ago. The memories I have of these trips are good ones, although they include details that I look at a bit askance now, like being in the back of my aunt's station wagon with a young adult cousin at the wheel, and he and my aunt and my mother all laughing, drinking martinis out of a thermos. At one point my cousin lost track of his lit cigarette, which blew back into the window of the car and burned him just as we swerved up to a toll booth. Ha ha ha.

Or an occasion when I was out past the breaking point of the waves with my mother and aunt, when I was perhaps ten or eleven, all of us with our bathing suits off, tied to our ankles, because they liked swimming nude. At a very public beach, even though we were far out past the other swimmers. It was indeed fun to be naked in the swells, bobbing up and down, and it didn't feel unsafe, but as I look back, it feels like a wrong thing to do with a child.

In last night's dream, after a lot of difficult driving, Dad and I were sitting on a dune very surprised at how large the waves were—truly huge—with

"All things shall perish from under the sky..."

tiny figures of surfers gliding along their crests, and also amazed at how high the tide was, how even on our high dune perch little waves were lapping at our feet. We were just watching the enormous waves and watching how close the water was to us. We wondered whether the tide was coming in. Even in the dream I felt that what we were watching had to do with him, not with me. The waves were not coming for me, but for him. Not here yet, but surprisingly big and powerful and surprisingly close.

***

Today Dad was going through old folders in his sporadic efforts to sort and throw things away. He was looking in one he keeps about the leach field and septic system, which hadn't been updated with any additional bills or notations after 2011. First he became convinced that the system hadn't been pumped out since then—but Allen said he knew it had happened in the past two years sometime. Dad didn't believe him and then went down a rabbit hole trying to figure out what various large payments in his checkbook had been written for eight years ago. He got very irritated and annoyed about it—I sort of recognized, intellectually at least, that what was happening was an anxiety state, but I felt impatient about the whole wild-goose chase. And all of this was happening at top volume since his hearing has deteriorated past the point where the current hearing aids can help him enough.

His search turned into him lashing out at me for paying Mary out of the wrong checkbook—he was really pissed off and I was quite blindsided, because I have always paid her out of the same checkbook, going back to last summer, and it is the one he told me to use. When he was really sick last July and I didn't understand his money system, I had paid the gardener and Mary out of the "unusual expenses" checkbook instead of the "regular expenses" checkbook and he had corrected me then. This time, he was very cross and said all the big expenses have to come out of "big and unusual expenses." I said that Mary was not a big expense, knowing that what he means by "big expense" is $500 for some plumbing or $600 for taxes and so forth. But he shook his head violently that I was wrong. Perhaps he is still struggling with his idea that the caregiver expense *is* a big expense. But the whole thing was very frustrating and very unusual, and left me with the fear that maybe we were entering a new normal, in which he would get paranoid about his money. But the next day it had all blown over.

***

Another bad night with him coughing and having pain in his side, but another night in which, thankfully, his pain and distress were resolvable with a lidocaine patch, some Tylenol, raising the head of the bed, and repositioning his pillow. But my pain and distress begin—figuratively speaking—once I've done all that for him. I wake up out of deep sleep, do what needs to be done along with Allen—with Allen doing most of this work actually, since he is the one who handles Dad's naked body and puts on the patch—but then once Dad is settled again, I can't get back to sleep for hours.

***

After two bad nights for Dad in a row, I woke up feeling cross and tired and out of ideas. Out of deep insights and deep thoughts even though, fortunately, I still feel the truth of this new phase for me emotionally—the realization that even if constant attention from me to my father would keep him alive, it is not something I can do.

Who I wish to be is the daughter who can hear his stories one more time, ask questions, enjoy jokes and shared time, and feel love. Instead I am the caregiver and the financial manager and the housekeeper. It will be much, much harder this summer when Allen is again offshore. Yet I am still in such a privileged position with all this, compared to so many other people who take care of elders, with no financial resources and no medical care in places like refugee camps and war zones, while also caring for children and babies.

This miserable feeling of being in free fall, with no visible bottom or landing place—this may just be the way it is going to be as I continue this walk toward death with my dad, with all my fears of my own death and with all my triggered states of yearning and loss and memory.

15

The Secret Place of Thunder

This morning I got impatient with my father as he once again overcomplicated something; this time, whether the envelope for his absentee ballot for the primary election would need to be signed "Ernest S. Hildebrand" or "Ernest S. Hildebrand Jr." I said I would ask the clerk as I wasn't sure whether I needed to sign the envelope too, since I was the one who had picked up the ballot. We'd had this same conversation at least a half dozen times over the past few days. This morning when he began to say he could look at some old documents to see which signature to use, I cut him off mid-sentence. He was justifiably annoyed at that, and said, "Let me finish!" I said, "No, I will not, it's just fiddle, fiddle, fiddle. I am going to ask the clerk and that will take care of it." Then I felt annoyed with myself for being so cross.

But I also felt, and still feel—when is it the other person's fault? Doesn't someone who is being passive-aggressive or goading or, in this case, just floating their anxiety at me (fiddle, fiddle, fiddle) bear any responsibility? And then I just felt sad. I don't think my dad could ever get what I was trying to say about process, which was, "Please let's keep this simple and relevant." And underlying that, although I didn't realize it at first, but could by bedtime when I saw how fragile I felt—"because I am at the very last strand of my ability to be patient with you and all this negative projection!"

This morning I see how fragile generally I am right now, and how much I am trying to balance. And I also see a deeper level to my part in the process. The life issue that extends behind, and ahead of, the particular circumstances I am in at this point in time. I, like my dad, have a lot of generalized anxiety, and my wanting to get things checked off a list in a simple way is probably a manifestation of it. Why should my need to cut to the chase in a conversation have any more weight than someone else's need to slosh around in it? And, there is no bad guy here, just opportunities to follow the spiritual path on which I wish to be and have chosen, which includes patience more than exactitude. My lack of verbal restraint comes from my buried, bubbling angers and frustrations. No matter how justified they may be, they are still not what I want to bring to the world.

***

I was doing pretty well with emotional equilibrium until last night, when seeing a yellowed piece of tracing paper which had slipped out of my father's old atlas, with a map partially drawn on it by James thirty years ago, made me deeply sad, missing the past. Talk about something little which bumps off a scab! An old piece of flimsy onion skin paper . . . Interesting to note that, as I write this, I can feel my fragility and how, if my father were to awaken right now and call out to me in his plaintive way, I would be so very annoyed. Would feel cornered and trapped and irritated. I am so sick of all these feelings.

I am reading *The Book of Joy* by Desmond Tutu and the Dalai Lama; but no matter what I do with their luscious insights or with quiet time or making gratitude lists, I come back over and over to this essential feeling of unhappiness. I know that caregivers often feel depressed, on edge, burdened. But it's not like I was living a happy, serene life before I started being my dad's caretaker. And maybe nobody is, and we all just show up as best we can, for all of it, all the time, anyway.

It's been a year since I came home from my job at the big hospital. My life, *my* life, is not about the job I had there, or about making contributions to research or to pediatric chaplaincy. Nor to having my ideas out in the world. Or about why people behave the way they do. I can see the futility of so much human striving all around me, every moment of every day, and I can see the tragic, horrifying ways in which people's lives are so much worse than mine. Children taken away from their parents at the border of our country and put in cages, all alone. Children and elders and women and men in war zones, in slavery, starving, diseased. My country and the wealthy nations of the world turning away from that suffering—and even worse, causing that suffering. I think, I hope, that when my dad dies, if I am still healthy myself, I will be more actively engaged in trying to change all these things. Maybe this is a time of preparation. Maybe my whole life so far has been a time of preparation. Or maybe not, maybe I will die without making any bigger contribution, without understanding anything more, without being happy consistently. People die that way all the time.

Yesterday Allen commented that he had not expected this caregiving gig to go on as long as it has thus far, and as it appears it may go on. That is true for me, too. After Dad's pneumonia last summer, right about this time of year, he was very frail for a long time, and then through the fall and early winter he seemed depressed, crabby a lot—perhaps getting used to and accepting his own decline. But now he seems to be on an even keel physically, although his cough is a lot wetter. He actually seems to be happy from time to time.

On this one-year anniversary of Dad's hospitalization for pneumonia, I can honestly say that I have made progress in being patient and forbearing with him, in detaching from his control, and from the impacts of my childhood. And I am almost at the end of my year of this writing, a commitment I made to myself on July twenty-eighth last year. But I don't want to stop writing. But do I really need to say over and over again that caregiving is hard, that I feel guilty or alone or angry?

***

The hillside I see from my window is very green now. Rowdy and untidy with the growth of bushes and grasses and young leaves on trees. The same hillside that I watched as it was crisping and baking into tawny brown last September and covered with white drifts this February. The trees on the edge of the hill against the sky that are so green now will flicker with sunset flame again in August's light. A year has passed, a year of seasons, a year of weather.

Nothing seems worth bothering with. The fact of death for everyone and everything makes life feel so pointless. Not only death, but so much suffering before death, so much suffering for entire lives, of people, of nations. The great spiritual truths that we must live in the moment, that we must not project the future nor brood about the past, seem so inadequate in the face of the pain of living. What gives pleasure goes so quickly, what gives sorrow lasts so long. Or so it seems, in this kind of mood.

I can see that the trees are taller. And in this new season of the year, they have strength and volume, even though we seem to be heading into a drought again. The hill where my grandchildren went sledding on waves of smooth white only three months ago is revealed as hillocks and bushes and rocks, waves of green and gray.

This is a rowdy season, and I am so silent.

> Ps 81:7
> In distress you called, and I rescued you; I answered you in the secret place of thunder.

The secret place of thunder.

16

The Well

2019

I AM READING A lot of old letters of mine; my dad saved every scrap of communication I ever sent them and I sent them a lot. The letters kind of freak me out, as well as make my toes curl, as they are so chirpy and shirtwaist-girlish. I know about the things I wasn't telling them, like all the drugs and drinking and promiscuity. It is odd to me to see how late in my adolescence I was still signing off "Wudge" and well into my twenties still writing to "Mommy and Daddy" with many declarations of love. Was some of it meant as a smokescreen? Some of it to convince them and myself that I was actually still the person they thought I was? I suspect that a lot of it was actually that I was very immature. Wanted their approval, wanted their nurturance. Since I don't have their letters, I don't know what I got back, if I got those things, approval, nurturance. Some of my replies in the college letters to their replies show that at least my dad was worried about me and my actions, as I very forcefully continue to state how right I am about things like the 1970 student strike against the bombing in Cambodia, or dropping classes, and my penchant for, as he put it, "collecting mixed-up friends instead of attending to your studies." A lot of ego and a lot of need for approval.

I am appalled at the enmeshment, or what seems like it—even though I recognize that an eighteen-year-old who went off to college in 1969 was generally less mature than an eighteen-year-old today. And I also can match the sentimentality of so much of what I say with what I would guess were repressed emotions of my own fear and self-hatred; as I write that, it reminds me of adult alcoholics I know, folks not in recovery or in very early recovery—where a cloying and immature sentimentality takes the place of actual adult feeling.

***

I decided to up the pace on the sorting of my own stuff. Dealt with my journals, shredding those that had processing/information/drama that I would rather keep in my own heart and not leave as a legacy. Doing that reduced them by two thirds. What is left is a decent amount of material describing my evolution as a person and my thinking about the world, if that would ever be of interest to anybody. It is still interesting to me, anyway.

I read in a letter of mine to my parents in 1977 the insight I'd had in a training session at the crisis center where I was then volunteering, that I'd never had a chance to be a child. The letter sounds upbeat, excited, and I somehow seem to believe that this business of not having been able to be a child had just sort of happened, that it had nothing to do with their way of parenting me—or that reading it might have an impact on them. Because I didn't save their letters, I don't know if they acknowledged any reaction to this "wonderful new insight" that so excited me. As I read over these old letters, I have mostly felt guilty at what I put my parents through, as I hopped around from conviction to conviction, idea to idea, relationship to relationship, not to mention geographical location to location. Just at this minute I can suddenly see that they had a hand in creating that . . . just at this minute I can see a source for my abiding rage . . .

Now I am looking over my poetry in a systematic way. I organized two manuscripts of it in the past, but there are many poems that didn't make it into either one. I plan to organize all of it that's any good into more books. And then maybe, maybe, start the trying-to-be-published thing again. Or just leave my heirs a bunch of well-organized writing. That they can throw into a dumpster—in a well-organized way. But on a morning like this one, when I feel so sad and life seems so futile, the sorting and sifting doesn't feel very meaningful and it is hard to think of any activity that would. Maybe there is none. Just put one foot in front of the other, trying as hard as I can to be as grateful as I can for what is, and not grieve over what is not.

The Well

***

Embarked on getting rid of things, and even with the luxury of doing it at a reasonable pace I still keep getting overwhelmed by the sheer volume of it. Yesterday, while communicating with a historical society in Connecticut that had taken a bedspread from the early 1800s from us a few years ago, in the hopes that they would now want a family desk from the late 1700s, I got into a tangle of little scraps of paper of my dad's—this time, scraps with genealogical info. Oh my God. Another thing to ask my dad about and try to organize, but, do I want to spend the time? Is it important? Will I be terribly sad when the book of his recollections is closed forever? But I can't live my life in the past of my family, I have to live in the now. And while it is anxiety-producing to do this review (will I regret throwing or giving something away???), it is anxiety-relieving to get rid of stuff. And then to not second-guess myself!

I am into my mother's boxes of letters, having dispensed with all of mine. My therapist said to me the other day, as I was exploring the ongoing process of sorting, saving, and throwing away, that to have an awareness of one's past, to be located within it, and to think of what one wants one's future to be, is proven by research to be extremely useful and helpful in making meaning of one's life. She also said that other research shows that doing that sort of work, maintaining that awareness of past and future is extremely anxiety producing. I can relate to both of those ideas. I find myself not discovering much, if anything, that I didn't know about my family—at least back through my parents' birth families, with their parents and siblings, a bit about grandparents and great-aunts, etc.—and being somewhat amazed at the power of the awareness. The Second World War was such a huge experience for the world, in so many differing ways, and certainly for my parents—their own experiences, their siblings' and friends' experiences.

Some of what I have been skimming and throwing away this week are love letters from many men to my mother from the forties, during the war and just after it. Or rather, "lust letters" from friends—this one writes from Cairo, that one from Manila, this one reflecting on how his experiences at Iwo have changed him, that one appalled by the state of things in Germany. But not very much about those things, much more about how they went swimming or drinking or wish they were home. Several of them write about the sex they had with her and wish they could have at that moment—as well as about the "girls" they plan to marry or have married. My mom was in her thirties, they were probably all younger than she—she described herself to me as "big sister" to the "lonely boys overseas." They appreciate her lack of neediness, her being such a pal, a drinking buddy, and so undemanding. It's not a surprise to read this, she told me these stories many times, and in 1996, when she was a hospice patient and we were going through one of her boxes of letters, we threw away many of this type, including nude photographs she had had taken for one of these men (she said, "I wonder who I had these taken for?"), and talked about her adventures. I remember how many times throughout my life, starting when I was fairly young—middle-school age?—she told me how sad she had been in her thirties that she was unmarried, how she didn't really take my dad seriously for a long time because she was nine years older than he and because she thought he was just another one of the "lonely boys overseas."

***

Dad had pneumonia again. Our awareness that something was wrong started the last week of May, because his right leg kept collapsing when he tried to walk. I called the palliative care nurse practitioner for advice on Tuesday the twenty-eighth. ("Sounds arthritic. Try a neoprene leg brace.") We went to see the doctor on call May 29. She also treated it as an arthritic issue and recommended physical therapy (PT) and a leg brace. We ended up in the emergency room that Saturday, June 1, and there they diagnosed pneumonia and admitted him. He improved quickly from antibiotics and hydration. PT began and the therapist said, "Don't get a leg brace! In most situations they are counterproductive!" With someone holding him up, Dad began to be able to walk and climb a few steps, and it seemed that the leg collapsing was actually secondary to the pneumonia.

Dad decided he didn't want to come home here and "be a burden" to me and Allen, and that he wanted to go to a nursing home. Even though I reassured him he wouldn't be a burden, I also knew how much more care he was going to need. So, we tried the nursing home. And the nursing home was horrible. Just as bad as everyone says nursing homes are, and way worse than I remembered this one to be from the days when, as their pastor, I visited people there. I took him out "Against Medical Advice" after a few days there—"Against Medical Advice" although the discharging nurse—someone who has known my dad for years, since his mom and my dad were good friends—quietly said, "Your dad doesn't belong here! You are doing the right thing!"

We brought Dad home to the gray area again—one day he is amazing us with his determination to get up on his own at night to use the commode by his bed, or to walk with his walker to the bathroom in the daytime instead of being trundled in a wheelchair—and the next day he is collapsed in his chair and states he is feeling horrible in a way he can't or won't define. Does not want to see a doctor but says he feels ill. I don't blame him for not wanting to see a doctor given what the last month was like—and I hope, I hope, he is ready to be admitted to hospice so that he can just stay home here and not be bothered by further useless medical interventions.

I had some really bad times in the past month—a little bit of the grief-feeling of "This is really going to be it, he is actually going to die" and a lot of the "When will he finally die, how much worse will it get, how much more will be required of us?" When he came home from the nursing home he needed so much help, and my days were defined by that. But, I actually rallied by focusing on gratitude, acceptance, and "One day at a time." I found myself one restless insomniac night thinking, *What does "after" look like?* And while there is some validity to that question on a practical level, on the spiritual level, I realized that there is no such thing as "after." There is only "now." That was enormously comforting. Take care of each moment and that takes care of "after." I was feeling that night like I was falling down a well, the well of mortality, the well of "What is the meaning of life?" the well of being born, living and dying essentially alone, within our own skin. Grabbing hold of acceptance, gratitude (even though it felt like an intellectual exercise at first, as it always does when I am in the depths of fear and powerlessness), and "One day at a time" brought me out of the well—or perhaps, made the walls of the well dissolve.

17

Enjoy the Now

First Sunday of the summer schedule. Dad is now formally a hospice patient, so we get more help than we were getting, including regular visits from a wonderfully competent and sensitive person whom Dad refers to as "The Bath Lady" and, as with his hospice volunteer, considers a new friend. I am amazed at his willingness to surrender his body to her care since he has always been so private, but she has won his trust. Allen has been offshore since Friday afternoon, and a new paid caregiver was here overnight last night. Seems like overkill to have someone overnight when I am here, and I hope that the money I will spend for these eleven summer Saturday nights won't one day make a huge difference in our resources, but it was so nice to just go to bed and not think about whether he was okay. Friday night I was very restless, trying to sleep and also be aware of him at the same time. But what I realized this morning as I put the bathroom downstairs back together for him (having moved the commode off the toilet so the caregiver could use it herself in the night, having put out clean towels for her that I don't want him to use, having put his gross toothbrush cup on the stand next to the sink instead of on the sink, and so on—as well as remembering to set out the breakfast things and the updated instruction sheet for the relief person who will come at 9 a.m. so I can go to lead worship at the church) is this is too much, almost. It is almost too much to add eleven weeks of Allen gone to the mix.

Enjoy the Now

***

So far doing this alone is going okay, and I have a sense of relief—only have to do this one weekend at a time, and the first one is down, ten to go. But ten weekends will take us to September, and I don't want to just grit my teeth and survive the summer.

I love looking out the window of my writing room and watching the gently sloping meadow and encroaching brush and trees go through the seasons. Right now it is all heliotrope, white drifts of blossom on long stalks swaying in the breeze. A splash of orange day lilies. We've had so much rain that everything is lush and green, showing no signs yet of the dry brown that I expect by midsummer. My little vegetable garden is delivering up peas galore and the first picking of broccoli. Cucumbers, tomatoes, and onions to come.

This morning Dad said he was awake in the night thinking about his brother's death a few years ago. I tried to explore what he was thinking about it, tried to delicately explore whether he was thinking about his own death, and, typically, he got irritated.

***

September. I am happy to say that I did not just "endure" the summer. It was hard, in the sense of balancing the church responsibilities with Allen away and Dad; I am glad it is over, but I did enjoy it. And I did have times that were meaningful with the grandkids and with myself and with Allen and with friends and in AA meetings. One thing that has been really nice is changing my daily walk so that instead of going up the road past houses and trees, I am going down the road and over the bridge on the Benjamin River. Crossing the bridge, I see that river and its many birds, the changing light and tides, and that feeds my soul in a richer way than the other walk, even though this route isn't quite as long.

I am more aware that Dad and I are not going to be partners in this enterprise of him dying. He's going to do it with all his customary anxiety about minutiae and avoidance of reality, and I'm going to try to be unanxious and as conscious and aware as I can. His path will include him fussing about not needing caregivers. Fussing about all kinds of little things. Being petty. And expecting that I should drop everything and do something for him *right now*, no matter what I am doing or that his stated desire is "not to be a burden." My path will include reminding myself of the primacy of meeting my own needs first, as best I can. And I need to stop expecting, hoping, looking for someone who can help me with this in some idealized way but to really, really, *really* focus on meeting my own needs myself, understanding that some of my yearning neediness is ancient stuff of mine.

***

Years ago, my son was an instructor at the Hurricane Island Outward Bound School off of Vinalhaven Island, and Allen and I visited him there. The generator for electricity was shut down every night at nine o'clock. Walking from the washhouse after tooth-brushing by candlelight to the small cabin where we slept, on one starless night I stood in the thick darkness, sensing but not seeing the shapes of the trees around me. There was just enough noise from the ocean and from the wind in the trees to block out any nearby sound. Standing there for a moment, blind and deaf, I felt a shiver of deep, primal fear—there on Hurricane Island, with my husband and my son in a cabin just around the next bend, and the woods full of sleeping teenagers on Outward Bound courses. Lying in bed later that night, I thought about my cat, all ten or so pounds of him: how he sits by the window at night with his tail twitching, hoping to slip through the door when an unwary human opens it; how he bursts out into the darkness, the master of it, in his element, on the prowl. Within that small befurred skull lies the self-image of a predator—and I have, despite my size, despite my opposable thumbs and my human ingenuity, on a very deep level, the ancient self-image, the ancient memory, of being prey. When I stand in the deep darkness, I don't think about the mighty deeds of humankind—the shudder that I feel is left over from another time, a time when humans, small and comparatively weak, lived surrounded by much bigger creatures, in an unsafe and unstable world.

You could say that one of the purposes of an Outward Bound course and other similar kinds of wilderness experiences is to encounter that shiver of fear, get to know it, work around it, work *with* it. The Outward Bound course in which I was a student long ago was a winter course in the Mahoosuc Mountains near Bethel, Maine. We climbed up a mountain, slept on its top with no tents or shelter other than what we made, and climbed down again.

Since I have a low body temperature even in normal circumstances, I was pretty cold a lot of the time. At night, we were instructed to put our damp felt boot liners into our sleeping bags so that they would be warm and dry in the morning; mine froze in the bottom of my bag. I learned that you can be so cold you think you will die, but not actually die. But the look of the nighttime winter sky from the top of a mountain far from artificial light more than made up for being cold. I felt a very muted kind of the primal fear. Just enough to wake me up to the reality of my tiny human life.

We may not all be afraid of the dark, but there is much else that we can feel afraid of in that deep, visceral way. No matter when or where we grew up, we all have plenty of the raw material for fear and pain. That does not mean that we live crippled by our pasts; on the contrary, most of the time we can function well, and cherish the gifts and the blessings of our lives as well as the challenges. But there are times that bring up our feelings of vulnerability, of being prey, such as times of personal loss like a new medical diagnosis, the death of a loved one, and the loss of home or job—and there are times in the life of the world when we are surrounded by big events, and everything feels unsafe and unstable.

Jesus knew our human vulnerability; he was one of us. When he was dying on the cross, he called out, "My God, my God, why have you forsaken me?"[1]—as we, in our times of despair, feel forsaken by God. A friend of mine with a desperately sad family situation said once, "I feel like we're perpetually living through Holy Saturday—we know so well the pain of the cross, and the resurrection is not yet come." The pain of the cross—what does that mean? The pain of the cross is the pain of human limitation, the pain of loss and longing, of seeing our very valid and beautiful hopes cut off. The nature of our lives as human beings is that we are all limited by aging and death, and most of us will also face circumstances beyond our control that will limit our fulfillment of our dreams. We cannot make our lives or the lives of those whom we love turn out the way we want them to in every detail. Our dreams will always be cut off, because our capacity to dream and to plan, to work and to hope and to love, is infinite, but our powers are not. It is only natural that we grieve and struggle against the reality of these limits, yet the fact that our ability to envision is infinite, while our ability to bring our visions to pass is not, is so profoundly and inescapably true that we must believe that that very state of limitation is part of the natural order of things.

God's physical world is a place of the finite. Our lives are limited, just as Jesus's was. There is a goodness in that, there is a goodness in the fact of our limitation. God made us this way. God made all that is this way. Even

---

1. Matt 27:46b.

the galaxies have a life cycle, a beginning, lots of change, and an end. Rather than adding to our despair by thinking that if we only try harder we can overcome our limitations or make situations turn out as we wish, we slowly learn that by acceptance we find God's grace and the courage to continue on. Does that mean that we are passive? No, that means that we embrace life as it is, with joy and gratitude and humor and courage where we can.

Jesus says, "Come to me, all you that are weary and are carrying heavy burdens, and I will give you rest. Take my yoke upon you and learn from me; for I am gentle and humble in heart, and you will find rest for your souls. For my yoke is easy, and my burden is light."[2] But Jesus doesn't only say those soothing words; earlier in Matthew's Gospel, he says, "Whoever loves father or mother more than me is not worthy of me; and whoever loves son or daughter more than me is not worthy of me; and whoever does not take up the cross and follow me is not worthy of me."[3] The whole picture is that it is in shouldering the cross of our limitations, accepting them, that we find easiness and rest. It is in this acceptance—of mortality, of our fragile and anxious humanness, that we are made free, that we become fully alive.

***

Dawn. Frost last night. Clear morning, pink clouds to the east, here obscured by too many trees, a hill, no open water such as we see from the porch at the cabin. But still beautiful.

> Where are the words? I want to
> Speak some truth
> About morning
> About death
> About dying
>
> October's first frost
> patches the still green lawn
> edged with umber, ochre, burnt sienna,
> palest yellow, pink-tinged brown
> as leaves dry out, as bushes turn,
> phlox that bloomed late magenta and lilac-blue and white
> zinnias the improbable colors of my granddaughter's crayons

2. Matt 11:28–30.
3. Matt 10:37–38.

asters everywhere, cosmos, calendula, bachelor's buttons
a snapdragon or two

brilliant friends
who kept me company through summer
as you coughed in the hot, dirty air
these friends
are dying.

***

I have had a very hard time being patient with Dad these past few weeks. He has deteriorated more, perhaps. A little more deaf, a little more forgetful, a little less steady. But he has also improved. Less coughing, less complaints about his bowels. Is that because of better medical management or a fluke? And oddly, even though I feel like lately I have been more snappish, when I think back to how I felt in July of 2017, I am no more angry and no less sick of being a caregiver than I was back then. If anything, I think I am actually coping better than I was. I have learned a lot, a lot about my enmeshment with my dad, about my own part in the passive-aggressive, codependent dance we do.

Perhaps part of my exhaustion now is that I am creating and maintaining better boundaries than I have ever had. I remember so vividly when, years ago, I dreamed more than one night about my responsibility to Dad, that he must never die, that it was my job to keep him alive . . . Now he is dying, albeit very slowly (aren't we all) and I am having to accept that I have "failed" and will fail to keep him alive forever. Not only that, but that there are limits to what I can do for his happiness and well-being while he is alive. I have been discovering this and incrementally living out the acceptance of it this whole time. I am not my father's keeper.

I have a kind of knee-jerk reaction so often that gets me thinking, *Oh, if I read one more caregiving blog*; or *When I finally get to a caregivers' support group*; or *If the kids/the friends reached out more*; or *If I were only more spiritual, then* . . . always this idea that there is something, somewhere, some kind of "more" that would help. "More" . . . the quintessential response of an addict.

While helping my dad take off his sweatshirt he elbowed me in the chin and I bit my tongue—not badly, but it did hurt and it startled me, so I said, "Ow!" He was contrite, immediately, and I minimized it because it was an accident. I said, "It is always hard when we are trying to do something together—sometimes I have hurt you, sometimes you hurt me." That's a pretty good metaphor for the whole damn thing. After it happened, and he was ensconced in the bathroom, I went to the big armchair in the living room—a retreat since childhood—and cried. Just feeling like I cannot do this anymore. But I have no choice. Or rather, no realistically acceptable choice. I'm not at the point where I am going to dump him in a nursing home whether he needs it or not.

On one level, what I have to do inside myself in relation to all this living and dying seems unbearably complex. Unmasterably complex. On another level, it seems simple. It is as simple as the fact that whether or not I am ready or he is ready, my dad will die soon. And whether or not I am ready or anyone else is ready, we all will die someday. So, there is nothing to figure out about it. The thing to figure out is how to live. That is actually much, much harder, and the two facts, the living and the dying, fit together. Any unpleasant, time-consuming task can be put off while you are alive if you think you have all the time in the world to finally get around to doing it. And that same task can be shelved permanently when you realize time has run out and you are dying. Or when you realize that your time is shorter rather than longer, and you begin to prioritize. It seems that it would be so much better if instead of brooding about death we all just got on with the tasks of living. The actual real tasks, like loving and forgiving ourselves and others.

18

Just Let It Go

2020

How can it be so long since I have written? We are well into January 2020 now. Dad's hundredth birthday was December 29, 2019, and we had a small party of friends and family. He was very stressed leading up to it, and tired after it, but definitely enjoyed it. Two days later everybody was gone and we had a rocky week—him growly and bored and lonely, me frustrated and sad. Then Allen and I went to Boston for a fortieth birthday surprise for James: seeing *Cats* with James, Emily, the kids, four college friends of James's, and Emily's parents.

I was in such a depressed, exhausted place going down that I actually didn't think I was going to be able to enjoy it at all. The drive on Friday was awful. I was cross and critical with Allen, kept apologizing, was projecting negative outcomes that the surprise and the occasion wouldn't be worth the effort. But by the time we got to Boston, checked in to the hotel, started connecting with people, my mood lifted and it was a very good weekend indeed.

Sunday morning we said goodbye, and Allen and I headed to the New Bedford Whaling Museum to donate an 1859 letter written to a relative of mine by a friend of his on board the *John Howland*, and an old piece of family scrimshaw. I called to chat with Dad and learned that he had had one of his uncontrollable bathroom episodes and was very upset, thought he should go to the hospital, and so on. I knew that it was 99 percent likely to be the same old thing—nothing—but felt that I couldn't really assess that from Massachusetts, so embarked on a frustrating time of trying to get hold of the on-call hospice nurse, trying to explain that I was asking for an assessment of what was up with him just in case it was a norovirus or something, trying to convince him to let one of the caregivers help him clean up . . . struggling with poor cell-phone reception and trying not to be impatient and annoyed with everyone . . . trying to figure out if I really should be heading back to Maine . . . thinking ahead to our trip to Quebec with James and family planned for February. Should Dad go to the hospital then for respite care? Should we just hope for the best? Should we not go? I was so frustrated that I felt like never going away again . . . but, we didn't leave, things in Brooklin got back on track, we had a nice time in New Bedford in a low-key way with a good night of sleep and a good visit to the museum on Monday, dropped off our items with a very enthusiastic and grateful curator, and came home.

Did I learn anything from it all? Well, I learned more about how to deal with hospice, which is way more bureaucratic than it was in 1996–97 when Mom was a patient, or in 1999–2003 when I was the chaplain for this hospice. I actually talked with the director, as the nurse told me that I shouldn't have called her since it wasn't an emergency. The director affirmed that I had absolutely done the right thing by calling the nurse, even though the nurse didn't seem to get that I was calling her because I had no way of knowing whether it *was* an emergency or not and I didn't feel I could ask the caregiver to make that assessment. If this were to happen again, I would be very clear that calling for a nurse's assessment is exactly the right thing to do and I would be more forceful with the nurse about that.

Oh, who am I kidding? I was perfectly clear and the nurse was a pain in the neck. She simply didn't want to go to Dad's house because the roads were beginning to ice up and she wanted to go home. But according to the caregiver who was with Dad, the nurse was very professional and good when she actually did arrive. And she was detailed when describing the situation to me afterward, although that was when she told me I shouldn't have called her.

When Allen and I got home late Monday afternoon, I was too tired and aggravated to be patient or kind as Dad and I reengaged and he was very full of his ordeal. I got (unhelpfully) cross with him as more details emerged—like that he had cleaned his bottom with the disinfectant wipes for the toilet instead of the baby wipes for his butt, and that he, unsteadily bending over and by himself, cleaned the floor—I just felt so frustrated and sick of the whole thing. Even though a little part of me was murmuring, as it often does, *Why are you letting yourself get so worked up about this?*

In any case, we parted for the night not in a great place with each other, but Tuesday I was able to apologize for being cross. And he was still so wiped out all day that once again I thought it might be the beginning of a new normal. He went to bed at six p.m. Tuesday night, and even though I always feel sad when he seems to be failing and get in touch with the vastness of the loss his actual death will be, I really, really noticed how nice it felt just to be able to go to my twelve-step meeting without being queried about it and sighed at with the corners of his mouth turned down disapprovingly. It was, frankly, a great relief, and I wish he would always go to bed at six.

***

Dad is in slightly worse shape, mentally. More forgetful, more confused. More negative, more fearful. I think because he can tell that he is deteriorating physically. No way that I can see to talk about death, dying, meaning, regrets, final words, blessings—any of it. Yesterday at breakfast he suddenly asked if he should change his will. Which is, I guess, a way of talking about death. But when I asked him what he meant, or what he was concerned about, it turned out that in the book about George Washington he is reading now, there was a section about problems with Washington's will—typical of Dad that something like that would cause him to be anxious about nothing at all, since his will is very simple: everything goes to me.

I asked if he wanted to change that. "No," he said. "But what if you die before me?"

"Then everything would go to James," I answered.

If this was a way of talking about death, which I think it was, it was an ineffective way of doing it. A dead-end, so to speak—because I don't know how to get at any underlying feelings he might be having related to the issue of "Who gets my stuff? Who will take care of my stuff?" I mostly try to reassure him that I will take care of it all, but I also point out, "We need to get rid of things because James and Emily will *not* want to take care of your stuff!"

I have been struggling with poor sleep and the heebie-jeebies that brings. Once I am awake, the anxiety starts. Sometimes it is based in the worries of the moment, and sometimes it is about the meaning or lack of meaning in life. The terrible, terrible losses of animal and plant life and some human life in the fires in Australia—a billion animals! Unthinkable. The rising tide of fascism worldwide. The stupidity of humans trashing the planet and each other. And then the microcosm: I read the websites about how to support yourself during caregiving and they always assume that you can rally a support system of people to make casseroles and soups, do errands, take you out for coffee, and the like. But I am not getting that! . . . except from Mary, and of course from Allen, my hero—although he may be in as bad a shape from all of this as I am.

One of the things that is so challenging and different about this end of life with Dad, as opposed to what it was like with Mom, is that I was not as immersed in either of my parents' lives before *her* death as I have been since. I knew many of the stories—especially hers since she was such a raconteur—but she didn't give me her journals and letters until she was at the end of her life. Reading through them after she was gone began my process of encountering her as a vulnerable, insecure, idealistic young girl and woman, born in 1911, who left home in 1928 to be trained as a nurse in New York City, had more than one heartbreaking relationship, supported herself as a nurse all through the Depression, and was a United States Public Health Service nurse commissioned as a nurse officer by the Navy during World War II. She met my dad, a Marine, in Norfolk, Virginia, when he was stationed on guard duty at the ammunition depot at St. Julien's Creek. They married in 1949, had me, their only child, in 1951, and moved out to the suburbs when I was four.

The woman I met in her mid-forties, when I was old enough to consciously perceive her, was not the same as the person full of innocence and yearning I met in those diaries and letters. And now I am sorting Dad's letters with him and seeing an idealistic, adventurous-in-a-quiet-way young man . . . with twinges of today's anxiety, to be sure, but, a different person.

Too much. Too much to feel such compassion and sorrow for them both, while trying to balance those feelings with the compassion and sorrow I need for myself.

***

I thought we had finished with the conversation about Allen's and my trip to Quebec. "I, Alice, am going to Quebec with my husband for a short vacation, and you have a choice to stay home with caregivers or go to the hospital for hospice respite care." I thought Dad and I had together decided,

Just Let It Go

for good reasons, that the pros and cons shook out to—he will stay here at home with the cat and the caregivers when we go to Quebec. But then yesterday morning, as I was walking through the living room on my way upstairs wrapped in a towel after a shower, he said, "Maybe the cat should go to Aunt Patty's." Which immediately got my back up as a few days ago he said we had no business having a cat: it was too much work. We were too old. And so forth.

I told him then that he could feel that and say that of himself but not about Allen and me. So, I wasn't sure if that was the tack he was on yesterday, but it turned out to be a different (ridiculous) annoying thing. I asked why the cat should go to Aunt Patty's and he said, "Because then I could go to the hospital next week."

I said, "But you don't want to go to the hospital."

He said, "That's because of the cat."

I said, "I can hire someone to feed the cat. The cat would hate going to Aunt Pat's, Pat has a cat, she doesn't need the care of another cat, our cat would feel scared and threatened," and so on. I basically just told him it was a dumb idea.

But I realized, in thinking about it more as the day went on, that one of the challenges evolving around me is that Dad is not quite a functional adult anymore. I have the garden-variety challenge of adult children with elderly parents, of seeing how I do indeed have to take away his personal power and make decisions without including him because he can't make good decisions and just gets more and more anxious. But the subjective layer is that I was trained by my mother (and by him too) not to upset him, which is nearly impossible. Therefore, I have alternately protected him (tried, anyway) and gotten pissed off and confronted him my whole life. Tried to make him be a grown-up, and then given up and taken over again.

I am still a child in relation to him in so many ways. Struggling to separate and claim my own adulthood. He has always added up two and two and gotten five or twelve or apples and train velocities. Not much pragmatism. *And* he has always surprised me with some underlying common sense at moments when I least expect it, so I am off balance, often. Part of why I was standing there in my towel getting mad at him was my desire to have a fight over yet another of his illogical ideas. I am intimidated by my dad and I also still want to fight with him.

That desire to fight runs very deep. The rebellion and anger that got me space and kept me alive psychically is what I am most in touch with. The anger at him for not being a different kind of parent is perhaps in there too?

***

Once during a visit with some lobstering friends, I asked them if their son was still fishing, or if he had hauled his traps for the year. They told me that he'd be fishing through the winter, saying, "Right now he's lengthening out." I could immediately envision what this meant: lengthening out the pot warps with extra pieces of line so that the traps could be set in deeper water, further offshore. When winter storms come and the waters grow more turbulent close to land, the lobsters head out. "Lengthening out"—in times of busyness and turmoil, when the waters of our own personal seas are stormy, or when the waters of the world lash against us, we need to lengthen out—lengthen our spiritual moorings. We need to set our traps in deeper water in order to catch spiritual food. This is what I knew I needed to do with my dad—lengthen out my spiritual moorings so that they wouldn't break and set me adrift. And this was also what made everything so hard. The need to do that, and my failures as I tried . . . I felt like Job, beset and bewildered.

In the story of Job in the Hebrew Scriptures, his friends, at first sympathetic, turn on him as he suffers. Since they are not the ones afflicted, they only have the patience to be supportive for just so long. They suggest to him that his sufferings are the "discipline of the Almighty." This is, unfortunately, a view of suffering that we are all too familiar with, although we don't necessarily envision God as the direct agent. "Blame the victim," it's called.

It is so hard to accept that suffering is just a part of life: aging, losing our grip, being a loving and frustrated caregiver, not being our "best self" to someone we love. When we can, we construct our daily lives as much as possible to remove any feeling of vulnerability. We look to science and technology, to money and mobility, to solve every problem. But sometimes, despite our best efforts, terrible things happen to us, to those we love, or even ordinary things like getting old. "It is God's will" has often ended up being the catchall explanation for whatever we can't figure out. But while the idea of something horrible being "God's will" may solve one problem, it creates another. How can we love and feel close to a God who causes suffering? We don't even like the idea that God "permits" it.

Just Let It Go

When we or those we love are suffering, we may find ourselves very, very angry at God. And our religious training tells us that that is not okay at all. So, we don't express it directly. It's just not done. We try to pretend. Even though we know that we could not be intimate with people with whom we are not emotionally honest, we think we can lie to God by being silent about our anger, and still feel deeply connected. We go through the motions of a religious life, wondering why God seems so far away and remote. We conclude that God is useless, that religion is unhelpful, merely a way of thinking left over from a more primitive age. And then we wonder why we feel such emptiness.

Job takes a different path, complaining loudly to God. Instead of giving in meekly to his suffering, he speaks up to God, he names God's behavior as unjust. Having lived as a devout man all of his life, he cannot imagine turning away but he doesn't mince words about his outrage, saying in parody of Ps 8,[1] "What are human beings, that you make so much of them, that you set your mind on them, visit them every morning, test them every moment? Will you not look away from me for a while, let me alone until I swallow my spittle?"[2] He speaks up, he complains, but he also expresses his faith; no matter what happens, he believes that at the end of it all he will see God.

The intention of the book of Job is not to explain why people suffer, nor to justify the ways of God with humanity. Rather, it is to explore the depths of faith in spite of suffering. Job's faith is not a quiet, inward thing, but rather a vital and alive relationship. This relationship is what is put to the test, and even though Job cries out against what is happening to him, he does not turn away from God, nor from his belief in himself.

Job comes to know God in a way far beyond what was possible for him when his life was smooth and easy. He says to God, "I had heard of you by the hearing of the ear, but now my eye sees you."[3] Job has been changed from a man who believed in God because of the religious traditions of his day, a man with a complacent and unquestioned faith. He goes on to say, "therefore I despise myself, and repent in dust and ashes."[4] The English translation does not have the same connotations as the original Hebrew; Job is not expressing self-hate, but rather his sense of his own smallness

---

1. Ps 8:4.
2. Job 7:17–19.
3. Job 42:5.
4. Job 42:6.

and seeming insignificance. Having had an experience of the being of God, the fabric of the universe, he participates for a moment on a level beyond his human limitations, and regrets his own struggling and complaints. It is precisely through Job's efforts to come to terms with God and with the tragic events of his life that he comes to the place of wholeness.

19

Pandemic

February 29, 2020

The day before Allen and I were heading to Quebec for two days with James, Emily, and the grandkids, while I was hurrying and not being careful enough, I got tangled up in the plastic we have hung at the foot of the stairs to preserve warmth and fell down the last two steps, twisting my bad knee and landing painfully. Took my breath away. And it continued to hurt, I couldn't put weight on it, basically could hardly move. Fortunately, the physical therapist I have been seeing since January for a chronic knee problem could fit me in with my now acute knee problem, and assessed that nothing was broken. Her assessment was that I had probably stretched, possibly torn, some ligaments. She did some ultrasound therapy and other soothing things, and told me to walk with a cane. In the night, it hurt so much that I felt like bailing on the trip. But I didn't and I am glad I didn't, because even though I couldn't do most of the fun stuff on the trip, I could at least watch.

I asked James if we would have any trouble at the United States/Canada border because of this new coronavirus, and he said no, the only question they're asking right now is whether you have been to China.

***

March 4, 2020

    I don't know why I still feel such a compulsion to write. After all these years of never getting around to being published, after destroying many of my old journals as too full of self-pity to want anyone to read after I die, I still feel guilty if I am thinking *thoughts* and not recording them in some manner. Now the news is filled with the new coronavirus, COVID-19; with the results of the Super Tuesday Democratic primaries; and I sit here writing in my father's quiet house. It is sunny and mild and very windy, and I feel overwhelmed with my own inconsequentiality.

***

March 10, 2020

    How quickly things in the world are changing. The new coronavirus is much more widespread, its reach into rural Maine feels inevitable. I don't even know if the grandkids will be able to visit here for a while, as youngsters seem to carry the virus whether or not they have it—so if they are the least bit snuffly, James may say they shouldn't be around Grandpa. I am on edge about it all—not so much for myself as for being properly careful for Dad. COVID would be a miserable way to die. And just wondering where it is all going, like most of the rest of the world.

    All I want to do is obsessively check the news to see what new terrible thing is happening, how close the virus is to us here in Maine (seven cases now). So much is closed. Will the closings be enough to protect the structures of our economy, of our healthcare system? Will there be an ending to this or will we live in anxiety while everything falls apart and the world ends? Is right now the "good part"? There is a lot I feel lucky about, in terms of having a warm, safe home, and a loving husband and a cat, and the beauties of nature, good friends, and a loving family who are good at taking care of themselves, each other, and their kids.

    But where is this all headed?

***

March 19, 2020

    So, this reflection, which I started in 2017 as a way to stay sane despite suddenly being a caregiver for Dad, is now a possible aid to sanity as we are "sheltering in place" during the pandemic of 2020. Possible aid to sanity, as it is so hard for me to focus on anything except the news and the *New York*

Times Spelling Bee. It doesn't help that my knee is still out of kilter. I had a cortisone shot on March 11—so glad that appointment suddenly opened up since all routine medical care is now shut down—and it feels much better with the inflammation reduced. But I don't really know yet whether there is some larger problem to contend with, like a torn meniscus, and I don't want to aggravate it.

I am annoyed by Facebook posts that act like this tragedy, at least partially caused by human overpopulation and exploitation of the natural world rebounding on us in a terrible illness, is a wonderful spiritual opportunity. Yes, we can respond that way, but to focus on it as *only* that kind of experience seems like the epitome of self-centered denial of how much suffering this pandemic is causing, and going to cause.

***

Once, long ago, when I was a student intern with the Protestant chaplain at the University of Maine in Orono, I went with a group of students to a Zendo, to sit *zazen*, to practice Zen Buddhist meditation. The Zendo was a beautiful building, lovingly made from fine woods and stone, with the spruce and rocks outside that are so much a part of the Maine landscape and yet manage to look also very Japanese. A quiet gray sky, a small pond dotted with gently swimming ducks, banks of carefully groomed moss and grasses, led us into an unfamiliar and wonderful world of silence.

The first thing we were taught before sitting down on our cushions was how to breathe—deeply, so that our breaths went down to the very bottom of our lungs and then out again, completely emptying. We were taught about breath, about breathing itself, and about how powerful just being aware of our breathing actually is. A Zen Buddhist probably wouldn't use this word, but as we focused so carefully on our breathing, I realized that breathing is sacred; it reminds us of God. To breathe, just to breathe, is a sacred act, for it is by our breathing that we experience the miracle of life, God's gift. In this time of coronavirus, it is breath that is the most compromised; the simple act of breathing which we mostly do unconsciously throughout our lives is become impossible for so many of those who are ill.

That morning we also learned how difficult it is to "just" breathe—just breathe and not think about chores, bills, responsibilities, pleasure, regrets, shopping lists, on and on, through all the minutiae of our brains. We were taught to count our breaths, "one, two, three . . ." up to nine, and then repeat, so that we wouldn't get lost and wake up to find ourselves mentally intoning "one hundred" while thinking once again about shopping, appointments, and other clutter. An invitation to single-mindedness, to openness, to the blanking out of the perpetual yammer of our selves. A chance to reverence the breath, so simple, so mortal, so holy. In Hebrew the word for breath and the word for spirit are the same. God says to us as to the dry bones of Ezekiel's vision, "I will put my spirit within you, and you shall live."[1] It is not a Zen sentiment, but we can say that our breath reminds us of the spirit of God within us. We give reverence to the breath, the sacredness of life it represents.

The prophet Ezekiel lived through conquest and exile. He was probably one of the leading citizens of Jerusalem, for he was taken away to Babylon with the first wave of captives in 597 BC, after surviving the siege of the city by the armies of Nebuchadnezzar. God tells Ezekiel to prophesy to bones, to dry and scattered bones, the bones of the whole house of Israel, the bones of the lost. He tells Ezekiel to prophesy to breath, to summon the breath from the four winds, the very edges of creation, that the bones might live. The bones are called up from the dry valley where they lie, and life is breathed into them.

It is hard to imagine a more powerful image of hope when all hope is gone than that. Knowing that Ezekiel prophesied to people in exile who had lost everything, who had suffered terribly, removes from these words any possibility of easy, "pie-in-the-sky" reassurance—God will make it all okay, kiss our bumped knees, and set us on our feet again, with a harp and wings, in a sweet heaven. No, these words are said to those who could not believe that anything would ever be sweet again. These are words about the awesome power of God—the God of resurrection. The words do not render all of these deaths somehow acceptable, part of God's plan; we read this scripture in a world where reverence for the breath, for life, is masked, blurred by wind full of ashes, where the living walk through dry valleys of bones. These are words that *do not* render death and suffering acceptable, but they *do* tell us that death and suffering will not triumph.

Traditionally the church has read texts like this one from Ezekiel and the story of Jesus's raising of Lazarus[2] as promises of resurrection, events that point toward the fulfillment of all God's promises, but what does that mean? Does it mean that Good Friday is just a set-up job—Jesus has to go through the motions of suffering and dying so that he can rise to glory? No, it does not mean that. The suffering and the ending that Good Friday brings

1. Ezek 37:14a.
2. John 11:1–44.

are real. The sacred breath is extinguished. The loss is real, is painful. Jesus suffered on the cross for the world. Jesus still suffers for the world. And we can only know that *he* is with *us* in *our* suffering if we can allow *ourselves* to suffer *with him*; if, like him, we can allow ourselves to suffer with the world. And from that, from *that*, God will make new life. "Prophesy to the breath, prophesy, mortal!" Speak directly to what is most elemental, most simple, most vulnerable. Speak to the spirit, by whom we live and breathe. Speak in the dark places of despair, speak *there* to the breath. The deaths, the losses, the suffering are not erased, denied, rendered acceptable, but in their midst is God and new life. In the midst of the horror is new life; not beyond, not waiting for us out ahead somewhere, but here in our midst.

We cannot fall out of God's universe; we cannot fall out of God. We do not need to cling to the hope of resurrection far in the future, at the end of time, after the whole world has gone up in flames. We can experience new creation here in the midst of the conflagration. Here in the midst of the valley of bones, we can reverence the breath, reverence ourselves and one another.

The truest thing we can say right now is that God has given us brains and hearts with which to solve problems and with which to care about our neighbors, and that is our job today. As our healthcare workers show up; as our teachers show up; as parents and children show up; as people post messages and funny pictures and songs on Facebook; as religious and political leaders show up; and fire chiefs and storekeepers and restaurant owners and workers of all kinds; retired people; elderly, housebound; young and getting things done outside—all of us, we will just show up. (And wash our hands and stay six feet apart!) God is alive and well and walking through the ruins with us. And will always be there, in the outstretched hand we give to one another. In the nighttime sky, in the breath of wind.

***

April 16, 2020

Maybe writing once a month is going to be the way I keep track right now. Interesting to read over what I wrote early in March and see how small the impact of the virus still seemed—and then later in March, how big— and now is it really, really big. In Maine it is still manageable and hopefully it will stay that way. But it seems inevitable that we will be living in lockdown and "socially distanced" for a very long time, maybe even the rest of my lifetime. I am not hiring paid caregivers right now; no hospice staff are coming. Last night this was a devastating and self-pity-inducing thought—I was able to contextualize it to the many other things that happen to people, some done by other people as in war, genocide, terrorism; some not, as in tsunami, hurricane, wildfire, flood. Pandemic. And, really terrible, dangerously terrible leaders who march their country off a cliff into an abyss that lasts for years—that has happened before too, and it seems that that is what is happening, although hopefully, hopefully, between the Constitution and the separation of powers, we will not have to be destroyed by one man's megalomania and the fawning sycophants who benefit from his "vision."

Caring for Dad without help from the healthcare agency is easier than I thought it would be—perhaps because Allen isn't gone as much. I feel more ready than I was ever before to have Dad die, partly because I am so sick of the caregiving, but also because life right now is so uncertain, tragic, and constrained. Having the responsibility of his care makes it all harder. Protecting him from a death from COVID feels so important. And perhaps not possible. And with so much death around us, it is easier to feel that his passing is a small and normal thing. Even a pandemic is a "normal" thing. We're subject to disease. Microbes infect mammals so that they, the microbes, can live. That's the story.

The biggest thing that comes to me over and over is the oddly comforting thought that endings are as much a part of life, or even of nonlife in the sense of the existence of rocks and stars, as beginnings and middles. My lifespan, any human lifespan is so short, and we over and over again mistake "middle"—adulthood—for the most important part of the story. We don't remember our beginnings, and "where we were before" is as mysterious as "where we'll be after." So, we focus on the middle, and mistake it for the whole. And grieve and mourn and rail against fate as the middle gives way, quickly or slowly, to the end.

I make assumptions all the time that the days ahead of me will hold opportunities to accomplish things, or to enjoy things, or to make apologies to people, or whatever else is needed. I indulge myself in resentment and self-pity and inertia, assuming there is lots of time in which to get around to being a different person. Then this pandemic comes along and shows me that that is not the case at all. Last night I felt so sad about the end of life as we know it, perhaps not to recover before my death, if ever—but then I contextualized it, as I said above, and also saw how very lucky I am, in part because I have the luxury of time for reflecting and thinking.

***

Pandemic

April 28, 2020

A really crappy day today, which makes me mad at myself. A month ago, we all thought we might die from COVID. So why can't I just be relieved and grateful? My emergency-medicine-doctor son is safe. At least for now; who knows about the "second wave" next fall. Now things are opening up, although that is very controversial—but still, "the curve" was "flattened," COVID never hit Maine as badly as it might have, and even though cases are still rising (1040 today) and fifty-one people have died, each of whom was someone's family member or friend, the pandemic isn't (yet?) the catastrophe that it seemed like it might be.

But, the cavalier way that folks talk about us old people still needing to shelter in place—while there was all sorts of extra attention given to how to homeschool children and how hard it was for parents trying to work from home with their young children underfoot, not much was said about how hard it is to be stuck at home. Or how hard it is normally to be over sixty-five and sidelined by the culture in the best of times. I get that it is a contribution to the curve staying flat for me to just stay out of the way, but, it fits so neatly with the ageism that assumes old people have nothing much to offer.

***

April 29, 2020

I have been a wreck these last two days. Mary says she woke up and screamed so loudly and long that it made her croaky for hours. I keep bursting into tears, not screaming, but I am irritable as all get-out. Managing to be patient with my dad, but not with Allen. Based on nothing except my inner state. I really couldn't tell you why, except as I took a glass jar from a stash put aside months ago for my granddaughter Kate, anticipating a project she might want to do with food coloring based on a similar project she did last summer, I burst into tears. Some of the tearfulness has to do with missing the kids, and with the sense of utter unreality about the distance from them. I know intellectually that plenty of grandkids and grandparents see each other less often than we do, even in ordinary times, and that James and Emily might decide to go live their lives somewhere else someday as Eben and Laura and Justus and Julie already do, and that Kate and Jack and Sadie and Lucy will grow up and leave home and make good independent lives (hopefully, hopefully, in the face of so much uncertainty, pandemic, climate change, political darkness . . .).

I feel like I don't have the necessary skill set for these times. But, I enjoy the fact that Allen and I have been making garden beds and planting a few things despite the cold lingering for so long this year. I enjoy the fact that we are in agreement about retiring from parish ministry sooner than we thought. I enjoy the fact that it is sunny today and Allen is turning the water on in the cabin. But everything, everything makes me sad.

***

May 2, 2020

In a crappy mood yet again. It seems as though a decent day, in terms of mood, is always followed by a bad one. Today is beautifully sunny and clear for a change, although cool and windy. James and family are coming for the first time since the beginning of April, for a brief, "socially distanced" visit—and I am in a bad mood. Maybe because I was in a good mood yesterday, and that was partly because I was so excited about getting takeout from a local restaurant, but it was just food, it wasn't life-changing.

What would be life-changing? For my dad to finally die. And for the pandemic to end. This time of opening up the economy again is another kind of trauma related to the pandemic. Because what does it mean, and how do we do it safely? There are so many people here in Maine who don't believe that there even is a dangerous virus. They think that it is just like the flu. Or that the pandemic is only happening in New York City.

***

May 6, 2020

Writing a bit more often, to what end I don't know. Except that I have the habit of being a writer, and so there you have it. I want to try to get my emotions in some sort of order so I can figure them out, but I feel confused and distracted too much of the time to do that. The visit with James and family was really nice and did good things for my mood. Dad sat out on the porch with us as it wasn't too chilly, and the kids and I found ways to play and relate that he could watch. He also talked with James and Emily a bit. But that night was terrible; he coughed all night long and didn't sleep well. The next night I gave him a quarter tab of lorazepam and he slept very well but, as has happened the few times we tried this before, all the next day he was floppy and weak and not able to function as well as he normally does.

Pandemic

Tuesday we had the hospice nurse come into the house for the first time since early March, since Dad was still coughing and now having the mysterious pain in his rib cage. Everything was fine. I was glad she came; it reassured him and it reassured me, since my fear throughout these two months of pandemic isolation with no eyes on him but mine and Allen's was that maybe there was something new and different this time—maybe there was lung involvement, maybe there was something that could be or should be done. No.

So, there's the outline of some of the events of the past few days—but how to outline the feelings? I feel sad, I still feel scared although not as scared as I did in March. I have a short fuse, I am crabby with Allen a lot, sometimes with others. I have moments of well-being and gratitude and self-awareness that is positive—of my coping skills, of my ability to stay in the moment, to be optimistic, to get things done. But I feel so sad underneath it all. Still have, along with so many others, that bewildered sense of *but where did this virus actually come from?* I know it originated in China; I don't mean "where" in a geographic sense, but in the existential sense of where in the order of the world, which didn't seem like it included things like this anymore, but clearly still does. It just happens that this is happening now, in my era, the same way a tsunami or an earthquake or a hurricane does. This is the way the world *is*. But no matter how much I remind myself of the universe being made up of things and processes that evolve—the universe itself being a thing that evolves—I can't get my mind around it.

I suppose this is why religions and philosophies come into being: they represent human thinking and willing, which operate on such a finite, limited, tangible plane, trying to come to terms with the infinite, unfathomable, unlimited (at least in the time span of human years) universe. What does it *mean?*

I think it is positive that I am more aware of myself as a unitary and solitary being who will die alone and who can't depend on others to make her happy, to ameliorate mortality, to provide constant bliss etc. I have moments of real clarity about how short life is and how urgent it is to come to terms with it on its own terms. Allen can't "fix" death for me, any more than I can "fix" it for my dad—although I am sure Allen would like to fix it for me, to make me happy, just as I have struggled with that deep, deep conditioning to do that for my dad. That deeper awareness of my own solitary journey through this life may be a "gift" of the pandemic, although I hate to talk about any gift in it, since there has been and will be so much suffering for so many. To make of that experience of others' a spiritual gift for me seems obscene. I guess I can just be grateful for the awareness without seeing it as a gift of this time. People grow through all kinds of horrifying experiences. That doesn't mean that that is the best way to grow.

***

May 8, 2020

Yet again I am wondering if we have turned a corner, if things have suddenly accelerated, if this is the beginning of the end for Dad—or maybe just the end of the beginning, which would be much harder. Harder because the level of Dad's discomfort with coughing, weakness, and bowels is pretty high—and giving him the lorazepam that makes him sleepy, even at a quarter of a very small dose, makes him unsafe for standing and moving on his own. So, much more hands-on than he has mostly been these last three years . . . and I feel, when we are in one of these phases, how weird it is to have the edifice of his life collapse around us.

By the way, when James and family visited last weekend, Kate used the glass jars in her play. Felt like old times. But what will the new times be? And when will they start?

***

June 9, 2020

Started the lorazepam at a quarter of a tab May 7 and had a few bad weeks because of it—*maybe* because of it? Or maybe just coincidence. He is declining but, since he eventually returned to a higher level of function, I think it was the drug—and now we have given him half a tab the past two nights as he is complaining again about not sleeping well, and has a similar level of dysfunction to a month ago in terms of greater sleepiness during the day, a flat affect, and wobbly unsteady gait. The good part about the drug is that he sleeps more and therefore is less needy.

The bad part is that what he does need, he needs a lot of.

***

July 14, 2020

This is supposed to be about caregiving. So, I will say that the whole process continues to drag on demoralizingly. It is not just the indignities and the futilities that my dad, the patient, suffers—but also the indignity and futility that Allen and I endure. Neither Allen nor I can be gentle and compassionate from the heart anymore, but just go through the motions of keeping Dad safe and clean and cared-for. Our own indignities and futilities. And none of my friends calls me to check in with me—they either don't call at all or call to talk as if everything was normal and it was "just" the pandemic that is stressful. I am about as sad and angry and despairing as I have ever been.

I know intellectually that everyone is struggling and doing the best they can, but I am just burned out. Sick of myself, angry.

***

August 10, 2020

Here we are in August. And things don't seem any better . . . except that I had one of those very fleeting moments with Dad—yesterday he said, "I am tired of feeling this way." And when I asked what he meant, he said, "Under the weather . . . I guess it is part of the age." I said, "Being one hundred?" and he nodded and smiled a little half smile. And he looked so sad. It was so much easier to be supportive and caring when he was real in that way than it is when he is complaining about the windows having condensation on them, oh, what does that mean, will they rot the frames, what should we do . . .

***

August 21, 2020

On Tuesday, with tears in his eyes, Dad said to me after the hospice nurse visit in which we explored how generally crappy he feels and how little there is that can be done about any of it, "I want to live for a while longer." Broke my heart. He reached out and took my hand before he said it. I held his hand and said, "I think you will, you are healthy in all the important ways, the nurse just checked it all out—and we will do our best to keep you feeling as good as we can." And he teared up again. Afterward, he seemed to be in slightly better spirits, which would make sense as a discharge of emotions is supposed to make people feel better.

Then Allen and I had two days away, this time including an overnight, and we both were amazed at how different that felt. We were only at the cabin, took no trips anywhere, saw no other people, had no razzle-dazzle adventures—unless you count a boat trip out to Isle au Haut for lunch. But suddenly I felt as if I could imagine a life after Dad's death, a life that would be interesting, that would still include adventures, like boat trips to Isle au Haut. I felt possibilities, whereas usually I just feel trapped and stuck and like there is no future to look forward to, what with racism, fascism, climate change, pandemic.

I thought I would be able to carry that into my being back here but once again, I just feel depressed. It is a gray, threatening sort of day and I'm feeling like I have nothing to look forward to, which just feels like ridiculous self-pity—but, it occurs to me as I write this that maybe one reason why I am in such a crappy mood this morning is that this is the baseline for now—it was masked by the joy of being at the cabin. Now that I am back here in this hot claustrophobic house, I am in touch with it again.

***

August 31, 2020

My therapist said, "Alice, you are a mess, and it is because your father is dying." That bald statement helped in some way. And I had some decent conversations with James about some of this stuff too. But, man, I wish my dad would die before this gets any worse for any of us. Today, Allen is in Bangor hopefully getting our new electric car fixed, and I am alone with Dad, who had an accident in his bed and is generally woebegone. "Bath Lady" is here now cleaning him up; and she could calmly tell him that, yup, he needs to be washed, when he wouldn't hear it from me. I don't really know what I would be doing today if I didn't have to be with him, but I would love to find out. As it is, I sort of go back and forth between bathroom trips and trying to find activities for him and trying to engage sensibly and caringly with his distress about how he feels poorly, but we have been here so many times it is hard to go over it again and again.

I guess the most important thing to record is feeling less distress than I have for the past few months. Less depression. Less anxiety. More acceptance. Is it because of the work in therapy or the conversations with James? Probably both, although I think the work in therapy is the actual, real foundation of positive change that will last. The conversations with James are vastly reassuring and hopefully continue to build our adult relationship, but if I rely on reassurance from him, I will continue to be subject to too much insecurity.

And so August ends.

20

Since I Am Alive Right Now

October 13, 2020

The pandemic continues, of course. Likewise, climate change emergency. Likewise, election season and posturing and lying and criminal behavior. And Dad's decline. And my own depression. I am a bit more clear, most of the time, that the solution to my depression and pain is not family or friends, or anyone else, really. That it has to come from inside of me. Because, since I am alive right now, at this time when the planet is under such duress and is transitioning to a new climate that may kill us all, thereby ending the human era, I have to be "happy" or at least "at peace" *right now*, with the way things are, because this is the beginning of how bad it's going to get, not the end point.

When Allen and I took our one boat trip back in August, out to Isle au Haut for lunch, to my amazement, once we were out in Jericho Bay, I felt my heart lift and felt capable of being optimistic about myself and my future for the first time in a very long time. That lift of heart is something I am hanging onto these days, as I am back in the place where I can't feel hope or interested in much of anything. Can't find a book to read or a movie to watch. But out on Jericho Bay I felt like I *could* reengage myself when I have discretion over my own time again. And at the same moment, I am aware that I have to do that as best I can now, all the time, since my dad could linger and linger and linger. And since my own future is uncertain too, by definition. My dad has lingered way past the time of his own joy and discretion over his own time.

He doesn't express much emotion, he never has, so I don't know how he is experiencing this. I do know that he doesn't want to die yet, because he has said so. Not sure whether that is more about fear of dying or because he is still so engaged with many things—family, politics, the cat, whatever is blooming in the garden, a good meal. But he is more confused and more and more frail, and still anxiously alert about irrelevancies.

I feel like I am in a boat that has moved offshore—and my dad is still on the land—for some reason it doesn't feel like he has moved offshore. His state seems as if it lacks motion, lacks volition, it is just something that is happening to him even though he would prefer it not to be. Whereas I do feel like I am making a choice—to move away, to move out, to move on. To move on to my own journey of dying, in a more conscious way, although hopefully I have many more years in which to work to be part of a good, or at least, good enough, future for my grandkids and their generation and the generations to come.

***

November 14, 2020

Dad died 2:30 a.m. on November 9. I was with him for all of it, Allen for most of it. At the exact moment when Dad stopped breathing, Allen was out of the room. It was extremely peaceful; he just stopped breathing. I could see the pulse in his neck beat for a bit, then it stopped too.

***

Sirach 44:1–15
Let us now sing the praises of famous men, our ancestors in their generations.
God apportioned to them great glory, God's majesty from the beginning.
There were those who ruled in their kingdoms,
and made a name for themselves by their valor;
those who gave counsel because they were intelligent;
those who spoke in prophetic oracles;
those who led the people by their counsels
and by their knowledge of the people's lore;
they were wise in their words of instruction;
those who composed musical tunes, or put verses in writing;
rich men endowed with resources, living peacefully in their homes—
all these were honored in their generations,
and were the pride of their times.

Since I Am Alive Right Now

Some of them have left behind a name,
so that others declare their praise.
But of others there is no memory;
they have perished as though they had never existed;
they have become as though they had never been born,
they and their children after them.
But these also were godly men,
whose righteous deeds have not been forgotten;
their wealth will remain with their descendants,
and their inheritance with their children's children.
Their descendants stand by the covenants;
their children also, for their sake.
Their offspring will continue forever,
and their glory will never be blotted out.
Their bodies are buried in peace,
but their name lives on generation after generation.
The assembly declares their wisdom,
and the congregation proclaims their praise.

***

April 16, 2021

The poem about my dad that I don't sit down to write . . .
and now on this April day when icy snow hisses
and east wind rattles the stiff old plastic covering our cracked window panes
I am even less willing to write it, to think it.
East wind, and I have spent the morning looking through *Ulysses*
looking at Caxton's woodcuts for *Canterbury Tales*
and reading T. S. Eliot, all in pursuit
of how to convey my father to the family, friends, comparative strangers
who will gather on a hopefully hot bright day next June
if the pandemic allows
and say some words and remember him

remember him and remember that we too will die
even the hot hopeful bright-headed of us
and the ones who perversely love raw wind, who claim it
who are always exhilarated, whose strong white teeth
bite into things and smile, those ones as different
from my quiet courtly father
as June is from April
let alone December when he was born and November

when he died. He died so quietly
gently, with only me beside him
my husband having left the bedroom momentarily
to put on his pants. The cat had roused and went briefly to her dish
the moon was down and I watched
as he drew one breath
and then not another
while a pulse in his neck
beat a few beats more.

One hundred years, nearly one hundred and one
of beating pulses, of breaths, of cats who come and go
of bedside vigils, of loneliness, of unanswered questions
of unquestionable answers, the truths of
conundrum
of metaphor of
loss. Darkness, light, darkness once again.

Sleep, beloved father, you who never could sleep well in life
sleep under the sleety sky and rainy drizzle
and the hot, bright-headed days.

***

July 18, 2021

    For the past twenty-four hours I have resisted writing about this. Yesterday, when trying to take a nap, very sleepy, very relaxed, I started thinking about the zinnias I had picked an hour before and made into a bouquet with some gloriosa daisies; and then I started thinking about how I had bought the zinnia seeds last fall, before my dad died, in case there was a run on seeds again as during the worst of the pandemic year, and I wanted to be sure I would be able to grow zinnias for my dad . . . and suddenly, the enormity of his absence hit me so hard that I was almost in physical pain.

    I felt myself unmoored, like a rope bridge over a chasm with one end undone and swinging wildly. I felt like strong wind was blowing me about. I felt the sense of being lost, lost in the universe and was so sad, missing him, missing my mom too, missing the past, missing myself—who I was, my childhood, all of it, the time that passes so quickly, the mystery, the mystery of loss and life and death; and the thorough, complete foreverness of my dad being gone.

It was not until just this moment of writing the above that I realized that even though I felt that terrifying feeling of one end of my connection to the world essence *gone*, the other end was still intact—and that is the end connected to Jack and Kate and James, my genetic future. To my son's wife, to my stepsons and their families, not a genetic connection but a profound one nonetheless. I wonder if I can feel that now only because I talked about the panic and the grief with Mary, with Allen, and went to two meetings. I feel grounded again, although the intensity of that grief and the experience of the loss was so powerful that it hasn't left me completely, that's for sure. Somehow the beauty of the zinnias, the richness of their color, combined with the sense of swinging helplessly over a chasm, and even in the terror and trapped feeling of loss, I was aware of the lush greenness of the world and the vividness of its flowers. Flowers that too will die.

In the midst of death, we are in life.

Bibliography

Alcoholics Anonymous: The Story of How Many Thousands of Men and Women Have Recovered from Alcoholism. 3rd ed. New York: Alcoholic Anonymous World Services, 1976.

Barrett, Lisa Feldman. *How Emotions Are Made: The Secret Life of the Brain*. New York: Mariner, 2017.

Bultmann, Rudolf. *The Gospel of John: A Commentary*. Translated by G. R. Beasley-Murray et al. Philadelphia: Westminster, 1976.

Carroll, Lewis. "You Are Old, Father William." In *The Golden Treasury of Poetry*, edited by Louis Untermeyer, 206-7. New York: Golden, 1959.

Edwards, Jonathan. "Sinners in the Hands of an Angry God." Modern Puritans. https://www.modernpuritans.com/sinners-in-the-hands-of-an-angry-god-jonathan-edwards/.

Egan, Kerry. *On Living*. New York: Riverhead, 2016.

Episcopal Church. *Book of Common Prayer and Administration of the Sacraments and Other Rites and Ceremonies of the Church: Together with the Psalter or Psalms of David According to the Use of the Episcopal Church*. New York: Church, 1979.

Fox, George. "A Gathered People." Quaker Faith & Practice, 1647. https://qfp.quaker.org.uk/passage/19-02/.

Hearn, Lafcadio. "Dust." *Atlantic* (1896) 642–46. https://cdn.theatlantic.com/media/archives/1896/11/78-469/131953156.pdf.

How Al-Anon Works for Families & Friends of Alcoholics. Virginia Beach: Al-Anon Family Groups, 1995.

The I Ching, or Book of Changes. Translated by Richard Wilhelm, rendered into English by Cary F. Baynes. Bollingen Series XIX. Princeton: Princeton University Press, 1967.

Winnicott, Donald W. "Transitional Objects and Transitional Phenomena." In *Through Pediatrics to Psychoanalysis: Collected Papers*, 229–42. London: Karnac, 1984.

www.ingramcontent.com/pod-product-compliance
Lightning Source LLC
Chambersburg PA
CBHW071433160426
43195CB00013B/1878